Inmates' Narratives and Discursive Discipline in Prison

The question of 'what works' in offender treatment has dominated the field of prisoner reentry and recidivism research for the past thirty years. One of the primary ways the criminal justice system tries to reduce the rates of recidivism among offenders is through the use of cognitive-behavioral programs (CBPs) as in-prison intervention strategies. The emphasis for these programs is on the idea that inmates are in prison because they made poor choices and bad decisions. Inmates' thinking is characterized as flawed and the purpose of the program is to teach them to think and act in socially appropriate ways so they will be less inclined to return to prison after their release.

This book delves into the heart of one such cognitive-behavioral program, examines its inner workings, its effects on inmates' narrated experience and considers what happens when a CBP of substandard quality and integrity is used as a gateway for inmates' release.

Based on original empirical research, this book provides realistic suggestions for improving policy, for reforming current in-prison programs engaging in problematic practices and for instituting alternatives that take the needs of the inmates into greater account. This book is essential reading for students and academics engaged in the study of sociology, criminal justice, prisons, social policy, sentencing and punishment.

Jennifer A. Schlosser is Assistant Professor of Sociology at Tennessee Tech University, USA. Dr. Schlosser specializes in critical criminology, sociological theory and qualitative methods. Her research examines the narrated experiences of prison inmates as a way to help improve current prison programs and policies through individual and institutional collaboration.

Routledge Frontiers of Criminal Justice

1. **Sex Offenders: Punish, Help, Change or Control?**
   Theory, policy and practice explored
   Edited by Jo Brayford, Francis Cowe and John Deering

2. **Building Justice in Post-Transition Europe**
   Processes of criminalisation within Central and Eastern European societies
   Edited by Kay Goodall, Margaret Malloch and Bill Munro

3. **Technocrime, Policing and Surveillance**
   Edited by Stéphane Leman-Langlois

4. **Youth Justice in Context**
   Community, compliance and young people
   Mairead Seymour

5. **Women, Punishment and Social Justice**
   Human rights and penal practices
   Margaret Malloch and Gill McIvor

6. **Handbook of Policing, Ethics and Professional Standards**
   Edited by Allyson MacVean, Peter Spindler and Charlotte Solf

7. **Contrasts in Punishment**
   An explanation of Anglophone excess and Nordic exceptionalism
   John Pratt and Anna Eriksson

8. **Victims of Environmental Harm**
   Rights, recognition and redress under national and international law
   Matthew Hall

9. **Doing Probation Work**
   Identity in a criminal justice occupation
   Rob C. Mawby and Anne Worrall

10. **Justice Reinvestment**
    Can the criminal justice system deliver more for less?
    Chris Fox, Kevin Albertson and Kevin Wong

11. **Epidemiological Criminology**
    Theory to practice
    Edited by Eve Waltermaurer and Timothy A. Akers

'Foucault famously traced the focus of discipline from the body to the soul, but in this remarkable new book Jennifer Schlosser clearly demonstrates that the real focus is now squarely on the prisoner's self-narrative. Through what she terms "discursive discipline" the prisoner must repeat the pathetic mantra that imprisonment is the result of "bad choices" and cognitive mistakes, thereby disrupting the human need to make our lives understandable and bearable. Anyone who works with prisoners will instantly recognize the truth and deep insight in Schlosser's masterful argument. It is, to my mind, the final word on "responsibilization" in the name of treatment.'

Shadd Maruna, Dean, School of Criminal Justice, Rutgers University Newark, USA

'Schlosser talks to inmates about their lives, crimes and needs for successful re-entry. This simple act sets up an eye-opening critique of an inexpensive, widely used and superficially appealing rehabilitative program that sets up inmates to fail. With its theory of discursive discipline and practical suggestions for better programs, Schlosser delivers an important book for those interested in prison studies as well as "what works" for rehabilitation and re-entry.'

Paul S. Leighton, Professor, Eastern Michigan University, USA

'With *Inmates' Narratives and Discursive Discipline in Prison*, Jennifer Schlosser demonstrates that the contemporary prison system not only locks away inmates' bodies – it locks away their sense of self within enforced linguistic regimes of individual choice and responsibility. Significantly, Schlosser in turn proposes alternative approaches grounded in attentive social research and progressive justice policy, and so offers us a fine work of narrative criminology that interweaves critical analysis and practical application.'

Jeff Ferrell, Visiting Professor of Criminology, University of Kent, UK

12. **Policing cities**
Urban securitization and regulation in a twenty-first century world
Edited by Randy K. Lippert and Kevin Walby

13. **Restorative Justice in Transition**
Kerry Clamp

14. **International perspectives on police education and training**
Edited by Perry Stanislas

15. **Understanding Penal Practice**
Edited by Ioan Durnescu and Fergus McNeill

16. **Perceptions of Criminal Justice**
Vicky De Mesmaecker

17. **Transforming Criminal Justice?**
Problem-solving and court specialization
Jane Donoghue

18. **Policing in Taiwan**
From authoritarianism to democracy
Liqun Cao, Lanying Huang and Ivan Y. Sun

19. **Reparation for Victims of Crimes against Humanity**
The healing role of reparation
Edited by Jo-Anne M. Wemmers

20. **Victims of Violence and Restorative Practices**
Finding a voice
Tinneke Van Camp

21. **Long-Term Imprisonment and Human Rights**
Edited by Kirstin Drenkhahn, Manuela Dudeck and Frieder Dünkel

22. **Working within the Forensic Paradigm**
Cross-discipline approaches for policy and practice
Edited by Rosemary Sheehan and James Ogloff

23. **Positive Criminology**
Edited by Natti Ronel and Dana Segev

24. **Inmates' Narratives and Discursive Discipline in Prison**
Rewriting personal histories through cognitive-behavioral programs
Jennifer A. Schlosser

Inmates' Narratives and Discursive Discipline in Prison

Rewriting personal histories through cognitive-behavioral programs

Jennifer A. Schlosser

Routledge
Taylor & Francis Group
LONDON AND NEW YORK

First published 2015
by Routledge
2 Park Square, Milton Park, Abingdon, Oxfordshire OX14 4RN

and by Routledge
711 Third Avenue, New York, NY 10017

First issued in paperback 2017

Routledge is an imprint of the Taylor & Francis Group, an informa business

British Library Cataloguing in Publication Data
A catalogue record for this book is available from the British Library

Library of Congress Cataloging-in-Publication Data
A catalog record has been requested for this book

ISBN 13: 978-1-138-06589-5 (pbk)
ISBN 13: 978-1-138-81423-3 (hbk)

Typeset in Times New Roman
by Taylor & Francis Books

Contents

Acknowledgments

This book would never have been completed without the help of some incredible scholars and friends. For the support they gave me so many years ago and for their continued presence in my life today, Gary Brock and Karl Kunkel have been incredibly influential to me. Their confidence in my potential and encouragement throughout my career have been truly invaluable. They introduced me to the discipline and taught me that sociology is not just an area of study, but that sociology is something you *do*.

For their commentary, suggestions, honesty and faith in this research from its first iteration as a simple, if not overly ambitious, idea to its early drafts, I will always be grateful to John Galliher and Wayne Brekhus. They inspire me to push the limits of critical scholarship and challenge me not to back down in the face of opposition. Their support over the years has helped more than they know.

Dave Brunsma, for his decade of friendship and his continued contributions of late night readings, honest yet sensitive suggestions for improvement and unwavering dedication and support, I am truly thankful. Even when it comes down to the wire, he is there with enthusiasm to provide a fresh look and enlightening perspectives.

I am also grateful to Jessica Wintringham for the time, commitment and unique perspective she brought to this project. Her opinions as a scholar and a friend have been immensely helpful. She kept this manuscript honest and challenged me to come back down to earth when I needed to the most. Mom, Dad, Christy and Alan are my cheerleaders, my therapists, my perspective and my biggest fans. Their encouragement and support are unwavering and their belief in me is inspiring.

Finally, I am most grateful to David, John, Robert, Jesse, Darin, Joseph, Sam, Mike, Jason, Paul, George, Bill, Darrell, Tim, James, Wayne, Chad, Alex, Andrew, Reggie, Ed, Jay, Brian, Aaron, Steven, Derek, Martin, Dan, Harold and William. I don't know where they are today, but I hope they are all home, continuing their stories through triumph, if not some inevitable struggle. I hope they have found a way to overcome the challenges so daunting back then. I hope they are in a better place in their lives now than they were when we met. I hope their stories today are filled with perseverance, happiness and victory. I hope, and I am grateful.

Abbreviations

CBP	cognitive-behavioral program(s)
CSC	cognitive self-change
DOC	Department of Corrections
MODOC	Missouri Department of Corrections
PWC	'Pathway to Change'
THU	Transitional Housing Unit

1 Introduction

Reggie is a twenty-four-year-old White man from a large midwestern city. He dropped out of high school in the tenth grade and has no plans to continue his education. Reggie was raised by his father and had no relationship with his mother. He is currently engaged to be married and has one daughter who is sixteen months old. Reggie first encountered drugs when he was ten years old and smoked marijuana for the first time with some friends who stole the drug from their parents. Since then, Reggie said he has done ecstasy, mushrooms, cocaine, crack, speed and meth. Reggie is currently in prison for violating his parole.

Reggie said his troubles began when he committed armed robbery at thirteen years old. He said he kicked down someone's door to steal methamphetamine and money. He used a gun to commit the robbery and served six months in a juvenile detention center. When he was eighteen, his sister and her daughter died in a car accident after being hit by a drunk driver. Reggie went to the sentencing of the man who killed his sister and attacked him in the courtroom. He was held in contempt of court and received two years of probation. After the incident, Reggie said he started partying, quit working and began doing drugs. He claimed that at the age of nineteen he committed fifty-three burglaries in one month at a local party spot. He said he had three partners in the burglaries but they all got off without conviction. Reggie said he did it for: "fun, adrenaline, the thrill and knowing that I was doing something wrong." Reggie served two and a half years in prison for the burglaries.

Out on parole, Reggie said that he "couldn't keep a job and still go to PO (parole officer) meetings," so he violated the terms of his parole and is currently serving ten months in prison. I asked Reggie why he believed he was in prison today and he replied: "I don't have a problem staying out of trouble, I got a problem violating on technicalities. I know I gotta do something different." I asked him who or what was the main reason he is serving time and he said: "back then, I'd say I was just being a kid. Now, there ain't nothing I coulda done about this time." I asked Reggie what it would take to keep him out of prison again and he said: "I think it takes somebody close to you to have a real conversation." Finally, I wanted to know if Reggie thought he would ever come back to prison. He replied: "it's inevitable, I'll come back on violations. I said what they wanted to hear. I said 'I'm an alcoholic' even though I've never drank. But I know I put myself here."

George, a twenty-nine-year-old White man, is from the inner-city area of a large metropolis in the Midwest. He dropped out of high school in the ninth grade and tried drugs for the first time when he was twelve years old. George said he dropped out of school because he got into trouble for truancy and fighting. George said of his troubles as a young man: "I was young and dumb, I guess." George would like to continue his education and get his GED.

George said that when he was growing up he lived with his mother, stepfather and three sisters. His mother did not work and the family lived on welfare. George said the most important person in his life growing up was his little sister, because he took care of her. When George was sixteen years old he tried meth for the first time with a friend. He said: "it wasn't as bad as I thought it was going to be." Soon thereafter, George began selling meth to make money. He claimed to make six to seven thousand dollars per week selling drugs. George said he knew selling drugs was illegal and "you're always looking over your shoulder" but "the money was addicting."

George said that when he was seventeen he was caught selling drugs and received probation. I asked him how he felt when he was arrested and George said: "I knew it was bound to happen sooner or later. I knew the consequences, I saw my uncles go to prison." Shortly after his arrest, George violated his probation by stealing a car. He is currently serving a five-year prison sentence.

When I asked George what he will do when he gets out of prison he replied: "I probably will sell again just to get back on my feet. I'll try to live a normal life and see if I like it. I'm tired of that lifestyle." I asked George what advice he would give to someone like himself and he said: "get out of it, it's not worth it. Money is not everything. When you're selling drugs, time flies by." Finally, when I asked him whether he would continue to sell drugs after his release, he replied: "the poor have no choice but to do this."

I didn't enter prison intending to examine policy. My research interests for this book originally focused on inmate identity. I wanted to understand how prisoners perform their various "selves" in the context of confinement. My original project focused on examining the coping mechanisms inmates adopted as a result of incarceration and how those mechanisms affected their likelihood of recidivism. I thought understanding the emotional experience of being a prison inmate would allow me to determine which in-prison coping skills would be most beneficial to them outside of prison. I was prepared for (and in fact, sought) all the gory details and knew that, eventually, I would hear stories that would make me cringe. I believed those details would tell me what the inmates were all about. Certainly, I heard some horrific stories; descriptions of rape (both committed by and on the inmates), pedophiliac fantasies, stories of drug overdoses, deaths of family members and details of violence and abuse. There were tears, laughs, indifference, anger and relief in the stories they told. Indeed, what I found during the course of conducting my thirty interviews with male inmates in a medium-security prison certainly touched on many of my original interests. However, the longer I was there and the more interviews I did, the more the shape of my research project changed. In an almost too-good-to-be-true revelatory experience, I saw grounded theory actually start to work the way everyone said it should.

Through the course of conducting my interviews, whether as a result of or in spite of the questions I asked, layers of understanding and patterns of prison life became illuminated in ways I never expected. The narrative nature of the interviews began to reveal a pattern among all the inmates' stories that was easy to connect. Each of them, through the course of telling me about their lives, seemed to be fighting against something in the words they used to tell their own stories. In fact, halfway through conducting my thirty interviews I realized that the emergent pattern was the way in which their stories all characterized an unresolved tension. On the one hand, the inmates poured their hearts out into the room when they talked about their lives as children, their neighborhoods, friends, families, addictions, loves, kids, arrests and dreams. On the other hand, they qualified, caught themselves, backtracked, justified and apologized, all at once. Woven throughout the narrative of life, arrest and incarceration, each of the men I interviewed eventually circled around to provide me the assurance that the reason they went to prison was a direct result of their *own choices.* Sometimes I asked why they thought they were in prison, other times they offered the reasons unsolicited; in every case, though, the answer they gave was ultimately the same: they made bad choices.

It wasn't long after I made this connection that I started to look for its source. As the interviews progressed, I began to speak informally with prison staff, probing them for clues without giving away what I had found. Soon, during a discussion with one of the guards about the inmates' daily routine, I discovered that all of them were enrolled in a mandatory, state-funded recidivism reduction program as a condition of their release. The program was called 'Pathway to Change' and its lessons were based on cognitive-behavioral psychology and the principles of Performance Theater. I wasn't told about this program before starting my interviews, nor did I think to ask about such a thing.

Upon learning about the program, I made the discovery that the 'Pathway to Change' course was not, in itself, the sole source of the inmates' discursive struggle, rather, it was simply one mechanism through which a much more pervasive and problematic experiment was being enacted. I found that an over-arching narrative, through the medium of the state, was working its way into the language of policy and practice in prison to form a meta-narrative of carceral control. The meta-narrative draws from the idea of perpetual individualism: that we (all of us) are entirely on our own to succeed or fail. In spreading this narrative, broad ideals of individuality, competition and singular responsibility take the place of unique experiences and promote a common way of thinking about one's place in society. The medium by which the meta-narrative is delivered is through the exercise of *expert knowledge.*

Inmates in these types of programs receive unquestionable "truths" from those who, they're told, know better than they do what's good for them, but who have also never really been in their unique social position. The story, then, is a broad tale that encompasses how they are able to think and speak about their place in society. A meta-narrative dictating how and what people ought to think and say, especially in ways that demand conformity and submission to those experts who know best, is nothing less than a mechanism of control.

When whole groups of people learn to abandon their own individual stories in favor of one written by somebody else, the effect is a unique phenomenon that I call *discursive discipline.* It controls how experiences can be articulated by rewriting them into a story that everyone can share. It changes the way agents speak of themselves and their lives, how they interpret the experiences of those who go against the meta-narrative and it limits how they are able to think about their ability to change the conditions of their confinement. Discursive discipline is the replacement of the unique individual stories of personal life experiences with a litany of common themes such as individualism, personal responsibility and the myth of equality. Inmates are told that these themes ought to be present in their lives and that their shortcomings are the direct result of not believing fully enough in them. They are, therefore, controlled by the threat of punishment lest they not accept this meta-narrative in spite of all the evidence they have experienced over their lifetimes to contradict it.

In conducting this research, I found that meta-narrative as alive and persistent as ever. The project of controlling individuality and the articulation of experience through discursive discipline takes place every day in one of our most modern social structures: the corrections system. Through my research, I found five patterns employing discursive discipline within the 'Pathway to Change' class, in the goals of the Department of Corrections and in the inmates' narratives. Across all the data sets, these patterns illustrate the discursive themes of choice, responsibility, context, goals and future. Each theme relates to a specific narrative purpose and is used as a guideline for how inmates are to act, think and speak of their own lives. In the 'Pathway to Change' class particularly, these five patterns are articulated through a number of other coercive codes. Within the program manual, principles of self-blame, degradation, disconnection, detachment from reality and expert knowledge characterize the oppressive expectations put on the inmates; program design flaws degrading the integrity of the program and the clear misuse of the tenets of effective cognitive-behavioral therapy.

A class called 'Pathway to Change' in one prison is the empirical focus of this book. The impact of that particular prison class, overall, is likely quite small, but what it symbolizes is one of the many ways in which discursive discipline is disseminated throughout our institutions of punishment. This book focuses in on that artery and examines its inner workings so the whole project of discursive discipline in prison, the forced re-writing of individual experiences into common themes, can be more fully understood and exposed.

Throughout this book, I will consistently use the word "inmate" to reference the individuals I interviewed. The agents of the institution call them "offenders." The presumption behind the institutional characterization of the inmates as offenders is that they have actually "offended"; through this, it is inferred that everyone in prison did something wrong. In that characterization, it is likewise implied that if they did something wrong, then they deserve to be in prison. It cannot be rightly assumed, however, that everyone in prison is guilty of "offending," and that everyone in prison deserves to be there. From the stories the inmates told, it was clear that being an "offender" is a title given to them by individuals outside their physical and social environments. Many of their stories reference actions they took that were based deeply in context, necessity, survival and experience. That they made an offense is a supposition imposed upon them by those in power. So, I chose to describe them as inmates of an institution, rather than as offenders to a population.

The inmates, however, refer to themselves as "offenders." They have taken on the label given to them by the institution and do not resist it. None of the men I interviewed questioned the word, but instead, used it consistently to refer to themselves and their fellow inmates. They successfully took on the language of the state fully and without question (Polizzi & Braswell, 2009). It is a similar process by which the Department of Corrections hopes to rewrite the life stories of the inmates; to impose upon them, through subtle coercion, a new story wherein they are subjects who offend the rest of us by making bad choices. Foucault (1979) wrote that discipline over the body is only the first step in the practice of control. To weaken the minds of individuals by encouraging them to become agents in their own oppression is the ultimate study in power. That weakening is precisely what is being done in prisons across the United States.

Looking back, I realize that what I originally wanted to study in prison was, in many ways, what I ended up finding. The skills inmates develop to cope with the experience of total confinement serve as a buffering agent between their "experienced" selves and the selves they perform inside prison (Gubrium & Holstein, 1998.) The problem was that I couldn't figure out where one ended and the other began. While working to negotiate their own storied lives, the inmates simultaneously embarked on the task of both subverting and accepting the meta-narrative of the state. The tension of discursively managing competing stories came to define their selves in prison.

The aims of this book are varied. First, it outlines the scope and the use of cognitive-behavioral programs in prison (CBPs). These programs have gained popularity among corrections practitioners, Departments of Correction across the world and scholars in criminology over the last several decades. There are numerous reports from academics and government officials extolling the merits of CBPs. This book examines the claims made by proponents of CBPs as well as the research and literature critiquing them. Second, this book examines two pieces of empirical data: interviews with thirty inmates enrolled in a prison cognitive-behavioral program and the content of an instructor's manual for that program. Here, the inmates' interviews are examined in juxtaposition to the content of the program to reveal issues of similarity and discrepancy. Third, in examining the convergence of these cases within the whole context of the emergence of CBPs, this book also identifies a larger, broader story articulating the tension and struggle inherent in the relationship of the inmates to the institution. While the findings from other research indicate that CBPs are effective at reducing recidivism, this book asks: at what cost? Here, a precise and specific working mechanism apparent to the postmodern condition present in our modern structures is exposed: *discursive discipline.* Constituting a habitus of cognitive control in prison, discursive discipline is the articulation of a general sense of confinement wherein the details of individual lives become inconsequential and the whole project of social control is enacted by the drafting of a common experience. The data here examine this phenomenon within the context of the state and its control over criminals; yet as we'll see, its articulation begins and ends with the will of the people. Fourth and finally, the site where these issues converge is a pool of information that, upon critical analysis, leads to the development of essential, programmatic reform. This book aims to provide realistic suggestions for improving policy, for reforming current in-prison programs engaging in problematic practices and for instituting alternatives that make more sense and take into greater account the needs of the inmates. The primary contribution of this book is that those suggestions for improvement are offered in ways that are more palatable and realistic to policy makers and corrections practitioners than other critical projects may have been in the past. Emphasizing a theoretically critical perspective to incite change is necessary, but packaging reform in ways that are practical and can be offered at no additional cost or risk to the institution may be most helpful in producing tangible results.

Chapter 2, *The engineers*, introduces and explains the scope of cognitive-behavioral programs in prison. CBPs are defined as mandatory in-prison intervention strategies designed to restructure inmates' thinking patterns under the discourse of rehabilitation. Chapter 2 outlines the boundaries, common qualities, goals and typical methods of implementation that prisons use to deliver CBPs to inmates. Sociological, criminological and psychological research is examined addressing both the presumed successes of and problems with cognitive-behavioral programs in prison. Meta-analytical data often show that the use of CBPs is related to a general decline in cases of inmates' recidivating once released from prison. However, qualitative in-prison studies indicate that mixed methods in the implementation of these programs may result in serious unforeseen problems for individual inmates both during their participation in the program and after their release. Chapter 2 addresses both types of data and situates the present study as one that questions the legitimacy of CBPs in prison.

Chapter 3, *Planning*, begins by discussing the theoretical origins of carceral control by examining postmodern perspectives of broad cultural meta-narratives.

Foucauldian theory is used as the premise upon which the concept of *discursive discipline* is expanded and made meaningful within the context of cognitive-behavioral programs in prison. Chapter 3 also addresses classical and contemporary literature in sociology that deals with social control and individuality more generally. Here, it is asserted that prisons are often used as laboratories for policies that have not been fully thought through or tested. Inmates are forced into mandatory psychological programs that may or may not have any real insight into their crimes, social situations or personal histories. Literature and research on the use of narrative methods in studying inmates in prison is reviewed and a discussion of the place of narrative in uncovering issues related to discursive discipline is offered. The concept of *expert knowledge* as a guiding force of the implementation of discursive discipline both in a broad cultural context and within individual prisons is explained in Chapter 3.

Chapter 4, *The architects*, further develops the concept of *expert knowledge* in general and, in particular, how it relates to 'Pathway to Change,' the cognitive-behavioral program in the prison where this research took place. This chapter uses reports from this particular empirical case to outline the state's goals and the program's basic tenets and empirically locate them as a source of expert knowledge. Empirical data are presented representing the position of the prison administration in the form of an instructor's manual for the program, as well as public statements made by the state, the Department of Corrections and the prison. Finally, the concept of *expert knowledge* is examined as the primary site of battle between administrators and inmates within the context of acceptable discourses in prison as well as the Department of Corrections and the taxpaying public it claims to serve. The question of who is considered an expert on reducing recidivism is raised as the boundaries of the debate are outlined.

Chapter 5, *The site*, outlines the area, history and location of the state and prison where this research took place, the scope and types of data found and the methods used to gather and analyze them. Chapter 5 also addresses specific methodological and research design decisions, the unique narrative analytical technique used during interviews and the drawbacks and shortcomings of the study. Chapter 5 discusses and explains the three types of data used in this study: 1) publicly accessible institutional documents from the Missouri Department of Corrections; 2) co-constructed narratives gathered during interviews conducted with thirty male inmates in one prison; 3) and the workbook and instructor's manual of 'Pathway to Change,' the mandatory, in-prison, cognitive-behavioral program the interviewees were taking at the time of the study.

Chapter 6, *The gap,* juxtaposes the 'Pathway to Change' class and the inmates' narratives by closely examining the empirical data to account for similarities and discrepancies between them. Three premises central to the development of discursive discipline in prison are discussed as they were found in the data: self-blame, degradation and disconnection. This chapter provides a comparative analysis that includes an in-depth discussion of the premises behind the forced rewriting of inmates' personal histories. The empirical mechanisms through which this phenomenon occurs are examined and their consequences discussed. Inmates' narratives are presented as they related to specific sections of the 'Pathway to Change' instructor's manual and serve to reveal the structural inconsistencies and the problems that emerge as a result.

Chapter 7, *The divide,* continues the comparative work of Chapter 6 but focuses on two final, broader themes found in the analysis of the program manual and inmates' narratives: detachment from reality and expert knowledge. These final premises are discussed in depth, and their problematic consequences are addressed as they are situated within the context of affirmative postmodern theory. The concepts defining detachment from reality and expert knowledge are identified in both the 'Pathway to Change' data and the inmates' narratives. These broad-based, structural problems are examined in the context of their shared meanings within the inmates' narratives and the class content, but also in the ways the program and the inmates' narratives diverge along these themes.

Chapter 8, *Crossing over*, identifies five additional, underlying patterns emergent from all the data sets. These five themes: choice, responsibility, goals, context and future, are common across every individual story, each Department of Corrections statement or policy and in every lesson of the program. The themes summarize the primary foci of the state and the individuals it controls as it links the guiding thread that both mutually connects and simultaneously confounds the relationship of the inmates to the meta-narrative of the state. Chapter 8 examines how the five themes persist across all of the empirical data sets, highlighting their interconnections, and constituting the impossibility of their separation.

Chapter 9, *Demolition*, outlines the context of the tension created where the cognitive-behavioral agenda and inmates' lived experiences clash. The idea that the institution creates a one-size-fits-all model of recidivism reduction is addressed and its dangerous effects on the inmates are examined by taking the realities of life outside prison into consideration. The theory of *discursive discipline* is further developed and its implications extrapolated out to reference broader cultural patterns. The battle over what constitutes expert knowledge is explored further, particularly within the context of oppressive forms of institutional discourse. In Chapter 9, the effects of discursive discipline for the inmates as well as the larger social impacts of rewriting individual stories into a common meta-narrative are examined. Finally, the processes of discursive discipline in other social institutions are identified through a review of pertinent literatures.

Chapter 10, *Rebuilding,* develops the notion of dismantling discursive discipline and critiques of the program are highlighted here. The model is shifted to examine what a recidivism reduction plan that centers on the inmates' contributions, as experts, would look like. Issues like relevancy, agency, practicality, functionality and personal investment are discussed in relation to how they could be re-introduced by shifting the model. Chapter 10 provides suggestions for real-world implementation strategies that radically change the current program in prison, but that can be achieved at minimal cost or resource to prisons. New policies aimed at reducing recidivism, in light of the present research, are suggested and outlines for actual changes that can be made at the institutional level are provided. The book ends with a conclusion providing a critical look at the findings of the research and how they can relate to other areas of analysis in sociology and prison studies. Inevitable drawbacks to the current project are addressed and suggestions for future researchers interested in examining policy and the tensions produced by the production of expert knowledge and the narratives of offenders are offered.

References

Foucault, M. (1979). *Discipline and punish: The birth of the prison*. New York: Second Vintage Books.

Gubrium, J. & Holstein, J. (1998). Narrative practice and the coherence of personal stories. *The Sociological Quarterly*, *39*(1), 163–87.

Polizzi, D. & Braswell, M. (2009). *Transforming corrections: Humanistic approaches to corrections and offender treatment.* Durham, NC: Carolina Academic Press.

2 The engineers

> "I don't have a drug problem, I have a money problem."
>
> James, 24

Systemic failures: the search for an answer

On July 18, 2014 the United States Sentencing Commission voted unanimously to reduce the national sentencing guidelines for drug trafficking offenses, applying the new guidelines retroactively for eligible offenders currently in prison. The implementation of the new guidelines made 46,290 prison inmates eligible to have their cases reviewed by a judge in order to determine their potential early release from prison. In making its decision to reduce the sentences of drug trafficking offenders, the Sentencing Commission cited the success of a similar policy amendment made in 2007 when it voted to retroactively reduce the prison sentences of offenders serving time for crimes involving crack cocaine. After the 2007 Crack Cocaine Amendment was applied, between 2007 and 2011, 16,511 cases for early release were granted (62.4 percent of the cases that were brought to court). The Sentencing Commission's follow-up study revealed that offenders who received an early release as a result of the 2007 Crack Cocaine Amendment were no more likely to recidivate than were offenders incarcerated under similar circumstances who served their entire sentence. The study broadly defined recidivism as "a re-conviction for a new offense; a re-arrest with no case disposition information available; or a revocation of an offender's supervised release" over the five-year period after release from incarceration (United States Sentencing Commission, 2014).

With these new guidelines in place, questions about what happens after inmates are released from prison once again come to the forefront of the debate on American incarceration and release trends. This important victory, supported by years of research and evidence makes studies addressing the experiences of inmates during their transition from prison back into the community all the more timely and relevant.

Yet, despite the efforts of the U.S. Sentencing Commission to reduce time served for drug-related offenses, most inmates, regardless of the crime committed, eventually recidivate. According to the Bureau of Justice Statistics, the most recent data indicate that between 2005 and 2010, two-thirds (67.8 percent) of offenders released from state prisons were re-arrested within three years, and three-quarters (76.6 percent) were re-arrested within five years of their initial release (Derouse et al., 2014). The fact that most inmates recidivate characterizes a failure on the part of the justice system to adequately address the issues they face after returning home. This failure to adequately address the needs of inmates post-release has been a topic of interest for scholars from a variety of disciplines for decades.

In the social science literature on prisons, there is much discussion about how and why the prison system is failing (Reiman, 1996). The failure is attributed, in part, to overcrowding, mandatory sentencing laws, insufficient funding and poor management (Lagan, 1991; Riveland, 1999). It's likely each of these issues contributes to the rise in recidivism; however, a more probing look at the relationship between the stated goals, policies and programs in prison institutions and the reality of inmates' experiences reveals a wealth of new information about how the system works, as well as how it fails.

Using theories of power, authority, domination, adaptation and coping to explain the experiences and identities of inmates and other stigmatized individuals is a long-standing tradition in sociology (Lemert, 1951; Sykes, 1958; Goffman, 1961; Goffman, 1963; Matza, 1969; Tittle, 1972; Reiman, 1979; Adams, 1992; O'Malley, 1992; Ferrell & Hamm, 1998; Bottoms, 1999; Liebling, 1999). Other researchers and theorists integrate state-facilitated crime and institutional rhetoric into empirical accounts of deviant behavior (Berk, 1966; Scott & Lymann, 1968; Marx, 1981; Skoll, 1992; Podgòrecki, 1994; Ewick & Silbey, 1995; Garland, 1996; Bosworth et al., 2005). Few have attempted analyses of those overarching, state-mediated practices and policies in relation to their presence or absence in the lives of prison inmates (O'Connor, 1995; Fox, 1999a; Fox, 1999b; Lynch, 2000; Rodriguez, 2003; Terry, 2003; McKendy, 2006; Paik, 2006; Bosworth, 2007; Inderbitzin, 2007). Even fewer have successfully integrated original empirical research concerning the accounts of inmates in a prison with those structural and rhetorical ideologies at the heart of institutional policy and practice. The integration of inmates' narratives with analyses of state correctional policy can best find its niche by focusing on a particular site in the fabric of institutional programming in prisons: programs designed specifically to reduce recidivism.

Recidivism reduction (or decreasing the likelihood that an inmate will return to prison once released) is one of the most frequently cited problems Departments of Correction face. The literature from corrections practitioners on the challenges involved in reducing rates of recidivism is vast and, because recidivism rates are consistently high, these practitioners continue to search for a cure. Over the last few decades, corrections professionals have addressed the recidivism reduction question by looking at the general process of reentry and offender transition back into the community. Reentry initiatives across the country have received millions of dollars in federal funding to create programs designed to facilitate offenders' transitions back into the community. In the sociological literature on corrections, prisons and criminology in general, scholars address the recidivism and reentry issue by looking at the specific programs used to treat offenders in prison in order to answer the question of 'what works.'

Cognitive-behavioral programs: research and critique

The question of 'what works' in offender treatment has dominated the field of prisoner reentry research for the last thirty years. Criminologists, psychologists and corrections professionals frequently argue that the current answer to the 'what works' question is: in-prison, cognitive-behavioral programs (CBPs) (Petersilia, 2004). One of the primary ways many state correctional systems try to reduce the rates of recidivism among offenders is through the use of cognitive-behavioral programs as in-prison intervention strategies designed to restructure the inmates' thinking patterns under the discourse of rehabilitation (Andrews et al., 1990; Petersilia, 2004; Wormith et al., 2007; Polizzi et al., 2013). These programs are typically centered on a group class environment, are often mandatory and always require the inmates' presumed internalization of the program's core principles as a condition of release. The emphases of most CBPs is on admitting responsibility for one's actions, avoiding 'victim-stance' and learning to recognize and enact healthy alternatives to crime and violence (Fox, 1999a.; Petersilia, 2004). The emphasis is on the idea that inmates are in prison because they made poor choices and bad decisions. Inmates' thinking is characterized as flawed and the purpose of the program is to teach them to think and act in socially appropriate ways.

Therapy-based cognitive-behavioralism asserts that distorted, dysfunctional thinking prevents the individual from fully understanding the consequences of his or her actions. Psychologists use cognitive therapeutic models to treat a variety of disorders including posttraumatic stress disorder, obsessive-compulsive disorder, schizophrenia, depression and personality disorders (Beck et al., 2004). Seemingly, the core principles of cognitive change programs make sense. The idea that individuals should become responsible for their own actions and committed to a crime-free lifestyle are appropriate goals. Further, a number of studies indicate that prison classes based on cognitive-behavioral therapy are somewhat effective at reducing recidivism, if done correctly (Andrews et al., 1990; Henning & Frueh, 1996; Wormith et al., 2007).

However, using cognitive-behavioral therapy in a group environment as a form of offender treatment requires making a number of problematic initial assumptions. First, it assumes prison staff members administering cognitive-behavioral classes and the authors of the programs are trained in the proper techniques of psycho-social group therapy and clinical diagnostics (Andrews & Dowden, 2005). In fact, in many cases the staff members leading group therapy sessions are trained to process intake papers, monitor complaints and requests, search for contraband, coordinate release dates and visits, enact discipline when needed and maintain the daily operating procedures of the institution. Prison staff members conducting group therapy sessions are rarely trained psychologists and are almost never licensed psychotherapists. Andrews and Dowden (2005) refer to the issue of proper implementation of prison programs as "programme integrity" wherein "a programme is conducted in practice as intended in theory and design, whatever the theory or methods" (174). In their meta-analysis of prison programs, the authors conducted a variety of integrity tests and determined that programme integrity is positively associated with a reduction in recidivism. However, the authors do not address programs in which the theory and methods of the programs themselves lack integrity. Deficiencies in the implementation of these cognitive-based programs are addressed without regard for tests to determine the internal integrity of the actual program material. According to Wormith et al. (2007), "much of the future understanding about correctional intervention is likely to come from moving beyond the simple, but important, treatment-recidivism study to the examination of in-program issues" (882).

Second, using a blanket general cognitive therapy class in prison to treat a diverse cohort of inmates assumes that therapeutic results apply universally across all class, racial, ethnic and age lines to treat inmates' problems effectively. Implementing a single, one-size-fits-all program without tailoring it to fit the individual needs and risk factors of the inmates goes against the evidence found in support of effective prison treatment programs, which emphasize individual assessment, risk-needs evaluations and discretion in inmate participation (Andrews et al., 1990; Petersilia, 2004). If such a therapeutic panacea were available, the issue of recidivism would be moot.

Third, these programs assume that inmates in prison all suffer from psychological disorders. Because cognitive self-change classes are not used with much discrimination, the principle behind their use inherently assumes that *all* inmates engage in 'distorted or dysfunctional thinking,' which is what has lead them to prison. With over 1.6 million inmates currently incarcerated in state and federal prisons, adequately thorough psychological screenings of each individual are impossible. As a result, prisons and Departments of Correction make wide-sweeping generalizations that all inmates suffer from distorted thinking patterns and reinforce a rational-choice model of individual responsibility, rather than examining the systemic and structure-based explanations for inmates' behaviors (Marbley & Ferguson, 2005).

Fourth, using these therapies in prison assumes that "curing" inmates of their problematic thinking patterns will prevent them from returning to prison once they are released. This type of assumption conflates recidivism with a disease that, with therapy, can be cured. The reality is that individuals recidivate for a whole host of reasons not adequately addressed by the prison system, such as poverty, drug addiction and a failing job market. Finally, inmates' completion of the cognitive self-change classes is almost always mandatory as a condition for their release. The coercion required for participation makes it impossible to tell whether the therapy works, or whether inmates simply play into the staff's expectations as they barter for their freedom (Stevens, 2013).

Cognitive-behavioral critiques in the literature

The enduring sociological critiques of cognitive-based therapy in prison are broad (Petersilia, 2004). Some research focuses on the ways in which these programs attempt to use expert knowledge to restructure the narratives of prison inmates in general (O'Connor, 1995), while other research takes us into a group class and emphasizes the unequal power dynamics among staff-instructors and inmate-students (Fox, 1999a). Still others focus on the discursive aspects of inmates' narrative storytelling and how they attempt to negotiate both a self-blame ideology and the reality of their own victimization (McKendy, 2006). Overall, the critique of prison programs like these spreads beyond specific cases to highlight, instead, a systemic meta-narrative manifested in the everyday practices of corrections professionals (Polizzi & Braswell, 2009).

Kathryn Fox (1999a) conducted her study of a "cognitive self-change" treatment group in a Vermont prison. Social control is defined by the program's insistence that the violent offenders participating take responsibility for their actions by admitting wrongdoing and by engaging in a self-change rhetoric. According to Fox, their active participation is evidence of the program's agenda to replace the inmates' subjective accounts with a dominant discourse that generalizes criminal motive.

Fox contended that the cognitive self-change program coercively redefines inmates' experiences by cloaking their rhetoric in psychological explanation; in doing so, the cognitive self-change program defines what is 'normal' and 'abnormal' for the inmates. When the inmates attempt to resist the program's conception of normalcy, group facilitators verbally shut them down. Inmates are made to believe their attempts to resist the group's definition of normal results from their 'distorted' worldviews. If the inmates continue to rationalize or justify some aspect of their selves, group leaders accuse them of not actively engaging in the process of rehabilitation. Fox (1999b, 94) iterates the core of these exchanges:

> Most inmates in CSC [cognitive self-change class] do not have violent self-concepts. The critical challenge of CSC facilitators is to convince offenders that these interpretations are incorrect, that their violence is not compelled but rather emanates from their own core pathology.

Fox illustrated the extreme tension experienced by offenders during group meetings. Inmates were asked by facilitators to tell their stories but were often "corrected" or "edited" when the story did not match the self-blame rhetoric of the program.

Fox contended that the language and stories inmates use to resist the institutional dialogue provides researchers with a new place to look to determine how power operates in prisons. The narrative nature of self-change groups provides a source of data that can reveal the often subversive, subtle coercions of the institution. Although the prison system in general is based on the use of coercive techniques, it is an overt process that is often overlooked as taken for granted by prison researchers. Examining more local exercises in power among the interpersonal relationships that exist within prison is a task for which narrative analysts are well suited. Exchanges between inmates and guards or instructors allow narrative analysts to tease meaning out of contested encounters in the prison setting.

Patricia O'Connor's 1995 study conducted in a maximum-security prison begins from the position that inmates construct agency on a continuum but that somewhere during the process of storytelling, they often experience an element of "puzzlement," or confusion, when asked about their motives. This sense of confusion is expressed in specific statements like: "I don't know why I shot him" or "I don't know what made me do it" (430). O'Connor made the case that in such instances the inmates engage in a "frame-breaking discourse," jolting them from their previously agentic story lines and forcing them into a subjective and reflexive moment of uncertainty.

When attempting to identify their motives for committing a crime, O'Connor wrote that inmates' accounts fall along a continuum. At one extreme, the inmates engage in "claiming," or the use of "I" to reference an event. For instance, the statement "I shot him," indicates a discursive moment of "claiming" responsibility. At the other extreme of the storytelling continuum, O'Connor indicated that inmates avoid claiming any responsibility and engage in "deflecting." Statements such as "we ended up getting caught" or "we had to exchange gunfire" are examples where inmates "deflected" responsibility entirely. O'Connor situated her current project in between these two extremes. The feature she called "problematizing" occurs when inmates engage in an active search for their own motives. Here, inmates experience trouble in the process of storytelling and search for the appropriate explanation of why they committed a crime but are unable to come to an adequate conclusion. O'Connor shifted the focus from the intentionality of inmates' actions and the agency they construct for themselves or that the institution constructs for them, and focuses our sights, instead, on the moments in talk that break frame, halt, puzzle, suspend and open up new possibilities for self-explanation.

Similarly, John McKendy (2006) conducted life-story interviews with thirteen men who were convicted of violent crimes at a medium-security prison in Canada. McKendy used the process of storytelling to determine what life events led his participants to commit the violent crimes for which they were serving time. He found that while the inmates told their stories they became torn between positioning themselves into the roles of either a criminal or a victim. Included in his article are narrative excerpts that illustrate the difficulty the inmates had in describing themselves as victims of violent, poverty stricken home lives and inmates in prison guilty of committing a crime.

For McKendy, the institutional insistence on inmates' admissions of guilt contributed to their difficulty in reconciling the two prominent roles of their life stories: victim and criminal.

McKendy's discussion of the inability of one of his participants to adequately negotiate the feeling that he was both a victim and a criminal is compelling:

> He works hard to artfully manage the tension or inconsistency between his ongoing discursive project of exculpation and the deflection of agency, and the requirement to position himself within the dominant discourse as a self-possessed responsible agent who claims his crimes (482).

McKendy used narrative accounts to argue against the "one size fits all" ideology of many cognitive self-change prison programs. McKendy concluded that in spite of the painful stories they told and their confusion and difficulty in having to speak of their own victimization as well as their victimization of others, the inmates were all able to express gratitude in being given a voice. McKendy concluded with the notion that the inmates' willingness to tell their stories, the catharsis they often experienced as a result, and the realities they helped reconstruct for themselves were positive outcomes of doing narrative methods.

In response to widespread critiques of current cognitive-based prison programs, Shadd Maruna (2008) and Alisa Stevens (2013) investigated how inmates can change their self-concepts positively in ways that help them desist from future crime. Using narrative and semi-ethnographic methods, both researchers conducted their studies in British prisons where advancements in corrections policy have skewed toward more rehabilitative, rather than punitive, techniques.

According to Maruna (2008):

> to desist from crime, ex-offenders need to develop a coherent, prosocial identity for themselves. As such, they need to account for and understand their criminal pasts (why they did what they did), and they also need to understand why they are now "not like that anymore." Ex-offenders need a coherent and credible self-story to explain (to themselves and others) how their checkered pasts could have led to their new, reformed identities (7).

The development of a "prosocial" identity, according to Maruna's findings, is in inmates' ability to take on "generative roles" wherein they locate meaning in their own rehabilitation. Generative activities for ex-offenders provide fulfillment, by giving meaning to future-oriented actions; exoneration, by absolving guilt for previous indiscretions; legitimacy, by becoming an active member of the community and therapy, whereby helping others, ex-offenders advance their own recovery (118–19).

Similarly, Stevens (2013) found that prisons using "therapeutic communities," where inmates use group therapy, positive self-talk, future-oriented scripts and mutual support, report a significant decrease in instances of recidivism. Shifting the emphasis from focusing on the negative aspects of inmates' pasts and the poor choices they once made enables therapeutic prison communities to create a safe space where a positive forward-looking orientation allows inmates to nurture a new personal identity. For both Maruna and Stevens, desistance from crime hinges on fostering a supportive holistic approach to understanding the self and the ability of inmates to change their identity and future actions.

Generally, studies employing meta-analyses use quantitative measures to address simply whether or not inmates participating in a range of cognitive-behavioral prison programs are more likely to recidivate after being released (Andrews et al., 1990; Andrews & Dowden, 2005). These studies report a statistically significant decline in those participating inmates returning to prison and so, to the question of 'what works' in reducing recidivism, the quantifiable answer becomes: programs employing cognitive-behavioral techniques. However, while meta-analyses provide information on the outcomes of prison programs in general, they are unable to critically address what actually goes on in these types of programs at the level of in-depth and specific program evaluation.

Researchers like Fox, McKendy, O'Connor, Maruna and Stevens who do go into the prison, interview inmates and pull apart the layers of prison policy and practice, are able to fill in many of the gaps left by those meta-analytical techniques employed in large quantitative studies on recidivism. The problem, however, is that both the broad quantitative studies and the specific qualitative projects examine only a part of the issue. The meta-analyses focus on whether or not inmates' engagement in certain programs will make them more or less likely to recidivate, but they don't tell us how or why this is the case. Qualitative projects focus on the interactional relations between inmates and staff, inmates and other inmates or inmates and specific prison programs, but don't adequately address how those interactions are related to other, more pervasive and expansive societal meta-narratives and mechanisms of control.

While the critical precedent is that sociological researchers believe the CBPs popular in institutional settings force inmates to adopt an ideology often at odds with their environmental realities, we must also address exactly what the inmates believe those realities to be and precisely where those divergences occur across a spectrum of inmate accounts. It is difficult to imagine critiquing such a widespread program based solely on the argument that reality is not being addressed without systematically determining where those gaps between discourse and reality exist to begin with.

To date, the most complete and detailed study addressing precisely this issue of identifying the gap between institutional discourses in prison and the lived experiences of the inmates is Jill McCorkel's 2013 book, *Breaking Women*. Drawing from ethnographic and interview data gathered over several years, McCorkel found that one particular program for drug-addicted women, called Project Habilitate Women, engaged in discourses that problematized the women's selves in order to "break them down" verbally so they could recognize their innate personal flaws. For McCorkel's participants, the humiliation and coercion required to work the program was almost always at odds with their own conceptions and interpretations of their "real" selves. As a result, they responded to the abuse of the program by either surrendering to the process, by "faking it" through until it was over, or by openly defying the counselors in charge. McCorkel's in-depth analysis of how Project Habilitate Women diverged from the lived realities of the women it claimed to help is a valuable study in how the exercise of expert knowledge is used in ways that neglect to account for the expressed needs of the individuals it claims to help. McCorkel provides insight into the juxtaposition of program language and methods with the narrated experiences of the inmates affected.

McCorkel's focus differs from mine in that she emphasized the role of prison privatization and gender in the 'habilitation' of women in intensive drug treatment programs, while my data focus on the relationship between the public and the institution in the programmed control and rehabilitation of men incarcerated for a variety of crimes, not just drug-related offenses. For McCorkel, 'habilitation'-focused programs start from the premise that participants are not whole people; that their selves are diseased, flawed and incomplete and that they will constantly struggle with becoming a whole person throughout their lives. On the other hand, rehabilitative programs use similar techniques to alter the "self," such as humiliation, degradation and coercion, but seek instead to normalize and responsibilize inmates through cognitive restructuring strategies designed simply to get them to *act* appropriately to avoid recidivating. Though our foci are different, the findings of our research on similar prison programs are closely related.

The process of coercing individuals to outwardly articulate their personal experiences in a way that matches a pre-approved, collective, manufactured narrative is a way of enforcing discipline through discursive restructuring. Individuality, uniqueness and varied interpretations of personal history are classified as sources of conflict and rebellion, which elicit punishment. Conformity, repentance and aligning one's ideals with those of the institution, on the other hand, are interpreted as behaviors worthy of reward. Discursive discipline is a tool of the institution used to streamline individual behaviors that are in keeping with the goals and agenda of the state.

Beyond the local: research and responsibility

The discursive restructuring of individual realities is not just happening in prisons and it is not a novel development. Disciplining people by forcing them to engage a common narrative and encouraging them to allow their unique experiences, struggles and perspectives to become subsumed under that narrative is one of the guiding principles of contemporary American culture. We encourage people to "be themselves" but punish (either formally or informally) those who are different. Discursive discipline is not merely a function of carceral control in the prison system, but a condition spread out among all of us and with which we are all familiar. Making the connection between the overt ways in which discursive discipline is enacted in prison will help to illuminate the covert ways in which the other parts of our social lives are likewise dominated. Bringing to light that connection is one of my goals for this book. The primary piece of empirical data I use to illustrate an overt case of the imposition of discursive discipline is a particularly egregious state-funded program being delivered as a method of recidivism reduction in prison. This case, in particular, allows us to easily see discursive discipline at work and I use it because the author of the program, the state politicians and the prison staff take no pains to hide it. Discursive discipline, in this program, is not hidden or deployed by trickery or covert means; it is evident, obvious and unapologetic. For those reasons, I have chosen this case as the vehicle by which a broader and more in-depth look at how social control through the imposition of a common meta-narrative is particularly enacted.

References

Adams, K. (1992). Adjusting to prison life. *Crime and Justice, 16*, 275–359.

Andrews, D. A. & Dowden, C. (2005). Managing correctional treatment for reduced recidivism: A meta-analytic review of programme integrity. *Legal and Criminal Psychology, 10*, 173–87.

Andrews, D. A., Zinger, I., Hoge, R. D., Bonta, J., Gendereau, P. & Cullen, F. T. (1990). Does correctional treatment work? A clinically relevant and psychologically informed meta-analysis. *Criminology, 28*(3), 369–404.

Beck, A. T., Freeman, A. & Davis, D. (2004). *Cognitive therapy of personality disorders.* New York: The Guilford Press.

Berk, B. (1966). Organizational goals and inmate organization. *American Journal of Sociology, 71*(5), 522–34.

Bosworth, M. (2007). Creating responsible prisoners: Federal admission and orientation packs. *Punishment and Society, 9*(67), 67–85.

Bosworth, M., Campbell, D., Demby, B., Ferranti, S. M. & Santos, M. (2005). Doing prison research: Views from inside. *Qualitative Inquiry, 11*(2), 249–64.

Bottoms, A. (1999). Interpersonal violence and social order in prisons. *Crime and Justice, 26*, 205–81.

Derouse, M. R., Cooper, A. D. & Snyder, H. N. (2014). Recidivism of prisoners released in 30 states in 2005: Patterns from 2005–10. Bureau of Justice Statistics; Special Report. Available online at www.bjs.gov/content/pub/pdf/rprts05p0510.pdf.

Ewick, P. & Silbey, S. S. (1995). Subversive stories and hegemonic tales: Toward a sociology of narrative. *Law and Society Review, 29*(2), 197–226.

Ferrell, J. & Hamm, M. S. (1998). *Ethnography at the edge: Crime, deviance and field research.* Lebanon, NH: Northeastern University Press.

Fox, K. (1999a). Changing violent minds: Discursive correction and resistance in the cognitive treatment of violent offenders in prison. *Social Problems, 46*(1), 88–103.

Fox, K. J. (1999b). Reproducing criminal types: Cognitive treatment for violent offenders in prison. *The Sociological Quarterly, 40*(3), 435–53.

Garland, D. (1996). The limits of the sovereign state: Strategies of crime control in contemporary society. *The British Journal of Criminology, 36*(4), 445–71.

Goffman, E. (1961). *Asylums: Essays on the social situation of mental patients and other inmates.* New York: Anchor Books.

—— (1963). *Stigma: Notes on the management of spoiled identity.* New York: Simon and Schuster.

Henning, K. R. & Frueh, B. C. (1996). Cognitive-behavioral treatment of incarcerated offenders: An evaluation of the Vermont Department of Corrections' cognitive self-change program. *Criminal Justice and Behavior, 23.*

Inderbitzin, M. (2007). Inside a maximum security juvenile training school: Institutional attempts to redefine the American dream and 'normalize' incarcerated youth. *Punishment and Society, 9*(3), 235–51.

Lagan, P. (1991). America's soaring prison population. *Science, 21*(5001), 1568–73.

Lemert, E. M. (1951). *Social pathology.* New York: McGraw-Hill.

Liebling, A. (1999). Doing research in prison: Breaking the silence? *Theoretical Criminology, 3*(2), 147–73.

Lynch, M. (2000). Rehabilitation as rhetoric: The ideal of reformation in contemporary parole discourse and practices. *Punishment and Society, 2*, 40–65.

McCorkel, J. A. (2013). *Breaking women: Gender, race and the new politics of imprisonment.* New York: NYU Press.

McKendy, J. P. (2006). 'I'm very careful about that': Narrative and agency of men in prison. *Discourse and Society, 17*, 473–502.

Marbley, A. F. & Ferguson, R. (2005). Responding to prisoner reentry, recidivism and incarceration of inmates of color: A call to the communities. *Journal of Black Studies, 35*(5), 633–49.

Maruna, S. (2008). *Making good: How ex-convicts reform and rebuild their lives.* Washington, DC: American Psychological Association.

Marx, G. (1981). Ironies of social control: Authorities as contributors to deviance through escalation, nonenforcement and covert facilitation. *Social Problems, 28*, 221–33.

Matza, D. (1969). *Becoming deviant.* Englewood Cliffs, NJ: Prentice-Hall.

O'Connor, P. E. (1995). Speaking of crime: 'I don't know what made me do it.' *Discourse and Society, 6*, 429–56.

O'Malley, P. (1992). Risk, power and crime prevention. *Economy and Society, 21*(3), 252–75.

Paik, L. (2006). Are you truly a recovering dope fiend? Local interpretive practices at a therapeutic community drug treatment program. *Symbolic Interaction, 29*(2), 213.

Petersilia, J. (2004). What works in prisoner reentry: Reviewing and questioning the evidence. *Federal Probation, 68*(2).

Podgòrecki, A. (1994). *Social oppression.* Westport, CT: Greenwood Press.

Polizzi, D. & Braswell, M. (2009). *Transforming corrections: Humanistic approaches to corrections and offender treatment.* Durham, NC: Carolina Academic Press.

Polizzi, D., Draper, M. & Anderson, M. (2013). Fabricated selves and the rehabilitative machine: Toward a phenomenology of the social construction of offender treatment. In B. A. Arrigo & H. Y. Bersot (Eds.), *The Routledge handbook of international crime and justice studies.* New York and London: Routledge.

Reiman, J. (1979). *The rich get richer and the poor get prison* (7th ed.). Boston: Allyn and Bacon.

—— (1996). A radical perspective on crime. In D. Kelly (Ed.), *Deviant Behavior*. New York: St. Martin's Press.

Riveland, C. (1999). Prison management trends 1975–2025. *Crime and Justice, 26*, 163–203.

Rodriguez, D. (2003). State terror and the reproduction of imprisoned dissent. *Social Identities, 9*(2), 183–203.

Scott, M. & Lymann, S. (1968). Accounts. *American Sociological Review, 33*(1), 46–62.

Skoll, G. R. (1992). *Walk the walk and talk the talk: An ethnography of a drug abuse treatment facility*. Philadelphia: Temple University Press.

Stevens, A. (2013). *Offender rehabilitation and therapeutic communities: Enabling change the TC way*. New York: Routledge.

Sykes, G. (1958). *The society of captives: A study of a maximum security prison*. Princeton, NJ: Princeton University Press.

Terry, C. (2003). *The fellas: Overcoming prison addiction*. Belmont, CA: Wadsworth/ Thompson.

Tittle, C. R. (1972). *Society of subordinates: Inmate organization in a narcotic hospital*. Bloomington: Indiana University Press.

United States Sentencing Commission (2014). Recidivism among offenders receiving retroactive sentence reduction: The 2007 Crack Cocaine Amendment. Available online at www.ussc.gov/sites/default/files/pdf/research-and-publications/research-projects-and-suveys/miscellaneous/20140527_Recidivism_2007_Crack_Cocaine_Amendment.pdf.

Wormith, S. J., Althouse, R., Simpson, M., Reitzel, L. R., Fagan, T. J. & Morgan, R. D. (2007). The rehabilitation and reintegration of offenders: The current landscape and some future directions for correctional psychology. *Criminal Justice and Behavior, 34(7)*, 879–92.

3 Planning

> "I don't think there's anything I could have done to stay out. The state likes to keep their hands around your shoulders, bobbing in the pool."
>
> Wayne, 27

A descriptive history: the origins of discursive discipline

In discussing the new "projects of docility" in the eighteenth century, Foucault (1979) referenced changes in the way discipline was being understood and used as a guiding force of social life. Foucault saw that the focus of carceral control had come to represent control of the individual body, rather than bodies, en masse. As a result of this shift, the everyday lives of people as independent, individually responsible cultural products became routinized to define the boundaries of control, regulation and structure without bearing the need for a singular, active agent or master plan. Discipline became the driving force of all social life at the consensus of the masses. Individuals came to believe self-control and self-discipline were the natural and rational means to achieving virtue and success. This shift in focus from an inter-dependent and socially integrated way of life to a highly individualistic and independent one indicated a new wave of mass governance. As Foucault noted: "many disciplinary methods had long been in existence – in monasteries, armies, workshops. But in the course of the seventeenth and eighteenth centuries the disciplines became general formulas of domination" (137).

These "general formulas" persist in our contemporary culture. We are no less influenced by them now than we ever were. If anything, the means through which we are dominated have simply become more streamlined, allowing the process of disciplinary domination to mask what Foucault called regulation and control and repackage it as independence, freedom and liberty. In fact, these guiding principles have become so ingrained in each of us that we now call them values. Each of us accepts these values as our own and we incorporate them into our life scripts. The tales we tell others and ourselves about our successes, failures, hopes and dreams all orbit around common themes. We have worked hard and disciplined ourselves in ways that make our accomplishments virtuous and praise-worthy. We script our personal stories by pulling from lines written in a common narrative. This method of mass storytelling, wherein each of us believes that the story being told is equally our own (despite any evidence to the contrary), is what Pierre Bourdieu (1977) called "dispositions." According to Bourdieu, dispositions:

> engender aspirations and practices objectively compatible with those objective requirements, the most improbable practices are excluded, either totally without examination, as *unthinkable*, or at the cost of the *double negation* which inclines agents to make virtue of necessity, that is, to refuse what is anyway refused and to love the inevitable (77).

Thus, the ethos of our modern social life is that which encourages, or rather *requires*, us to accept that our potential for action is limited in ways that we come to appreciate and even value. So, if we fail to achieve a goal we had set, our disposition is to keep our justifications for our failure within the acceptable vocabulary dictated to us by the ethos of our disciplinary life. We, in fact, do this willingly and believe unquestioningly that the limits to how we may conceptualize our own actions are entirely natural and good. In this way, Foucault's concept of the disciplinary nature of social life as the dominant perspective guiding the masses allows us to understand these formulas of domination as texts. The virtue and necessity of self-regulation through internally disciplining ourselves is a persistent meta-narrative that dominates how each of us is able to speak of ourselves, and our own behaviors (Schlosser, 2013).

When speaking of ourselves and our behaviors, we are socialized to use a particular vocabulary not only to express our successes, but also the rationalizations and motivations for our failures. Using phrases such as "it was my fault" or "I take responsibility" hold much more social value in our contemporary culture than do phrases such as "I couldn't help it" or "I didn't mean to." Agents in our culture who do not accept the dominant meta-narrative of excessive individualism and personal blame for failure, are seen by the rest of us as incapable of self-control. Because the narrative of blame, responsibility and restraint is so widely accepted as the unquestioned reality of living a "good" life, our cultural response to those who do not or *cannot* accept this meta-narrative as their own is that they must be taught to re-write their own experiences and behaviors in ways that compliment it (Maruna, 2008). We impute onto those who deviate from the meta-narrative a set of mental and social disorders. We insist that if they cannot speak of their lives using the language and text of the dominant discourse, then they must remain in captivity until they can (Fox, 1999a, 1999b; McKendy, 2006; Paik, 2006; Bosworth, 2007).

For Foucault, the project of control in the prison reflected a massive shift in the way the society was structured; today, the shift is complete. Now, rather than extrapolating out the processes of discipline and domination from monasteries, prisons and armies to the general population, we do the reverse. In contemporary social life, a denial of the general principles of individuality and personal investment in oneself results in excommunication to institutions where those principles can be taught. It is assumed that if an individual does not accept the meta-narrative as the rest of us do, we must first punish him for his digressions and then reshape his flawed thinking so that we may correct his pathology (Fox, 1999b; Reiman, 2009).

The basis of popular cognitive-behavioral classes used in prisons is premised entirely upon these principles of self-domination. What Foucault saw in monasteries and reformatories as men and boys practiced the routine of total confinement through self-regulation, happens in prisons still today. When individuals deviate from the laws of a society, we call them criminals. Prisons serve as "corrective" institutions designed to punish those who have deviated and (in theory) correct their cognitive flaws through discursive restructuring so they may be released back into society. Somewhere along the lines, though, the reasons for and motivations behind the commission of the initial crime become muddied. Once in prison, deviants are stripped of the uniqueness and truth inherent in their deviancy and are made to rewrite their experiences in ways that satisfy the dominant social and institutional narrative (Fox 1999a, 1999b; Paik, 2006; Bosworth, 2007). If they hope to be released from prison, the deviants must constrain their voices and behaviors within the boundaries of an acceptable and regulated discourse. Failure to accept the discourse results in an extended incarceration. So, in making the acceptance of the common narrative mandatory, the institution effectively makes any rejection of that narrative a crime in itself. In this way, the inmates are primarily disciplined for deviating from the law to begin with and secondarily disciplined if they refuse to incorporate the dominant discourse into the vocabularies they use to speak of their own experiences.

Deviants: resisting the meta-narrative and other such crimes

The idea that deviance is socially constructed, rather than a natural and objective force internal to the individual, is the driving conceptual paradigm that pushed positivism to the sidelines and opened up whole new ways of looking at differences in human social behavior. Indeed:

> if there is to be a field of inquiry called 'deviance,' it is social deviants as here defined that would presumably constitute its core. Prostitutes, drug addicts, delinquents, criminals, jazz musicians, bohemians, gypsies, carnival workers, hobos, winos, show people, full time gamblers, beach dwellers, homosexuals and the urban unrepentant poor (Goffman, 1963, 143–4).

To Goffman's long list of "deviants" I add: prison inmates. For as much as Erving Goffman contributed to the field of sociology and, in particular, to the study of deviance, he neglected an important component in the discussion of deviant behavior: the critical evaluation of the deviant individual as a potential source of institutional change. Other classical researchers (Sorensen, 1950; Sykes, 1958; Becker, 1963) similarly take interest in the deviant's account but focus primarily on how their difference from others carves out a unique place for them in social life, inherently separating them from "normals." These studies seem to imply that the stories of individuals considered marginal, stigmatized, deviant or criminal are useful only if they tell us why these people are different to begin with. The focus is typically on uncovering the deviant's motives for committing criminal or adverse activity so researchers can better understand what caused them to act the way they did (Lemert, 1951; Matza, 1969). However, in treating prison inmates as "deviant," or outside the realm of general acceptability, researchers manage to reinforce their subjects' social dislocation and enhance their further marginalization instead of working alongside their subjects to help locate a more liberating social position (Smith, 1999).

In response to classical criminology some studies take up the investigation of inmates in prison not with the purpose of determining what causes them to commit crimes, but to discover how inmates conceive of *themselves* as members of a community, rather than as socially doomed outsiders (Benaquisto & Freed, 1996). This trend in the social control literature is coupled with the methodological standpoint that emphasizes finding meaning in the marginalized stories and subjective narratives of "deviants" themselves (Crites, 1971; Bruner, 1991; Somers, 1994; Thoits, 1995; Gudmundsdottir, 1996; Polkinghorne, 1996; Gubrium & Holstein, 1998; Liebling, 1999; Maines, 2000; Denzin, 2001).

In her incredibly revealing work with currently and previously incarcerated African-American women, Paula C. Johnson (2003) looked to the "life history" accounts she gathered during interviews with twenty-three participants as a way to best articulate the realities of life surrounding incarceration. Using Black feminist methodologies and analyses, Johnson employed narrative as a way to articulate and make relevant the unique experiences her participants endured before, during and after incarceration as a reflection of the problems inherent in the criminal justice system. Similarly, Karlene Faith and Anne Near's (2006) book *13 Women: Parables From Prison*, used life history and narrative methodologies to present the stories of women in prison. These stories highlighted the vast inequalities endemic in the criminal justice system as a way to "humanize" their authors.

Other important research emphasizes the role of inmates' personal narratives in contributing to our understanding of the widespread, and often faulty, characterization of inmates throughout the criminal justice system. Diana Medlicott (2001) juxtaposed the narratives of suicidal male prisoners to the insensitivity rampant in prisons and mainstream culture about inmates' suicides. Lois Presser (2008) analyzed the discursive positioning of violent male offenders' narratives to better understand how they articulated identity in prison and how their self-conceptions were influenced by the workings of the criminal justice system.

Narrative methods and analyses allow researchers to move beyond reiterating their participants' obvious marginalization. Indeed, "prison is not a uniform experience. Studies have tended to take large undifferentiated samples and look for general patterns that omit the experience of particular groups and individuals" (Liebling, 1999, 7). In doing so, researchers miss an opportunity to become engaged in the social situations of their participants and work together to find meaning within those situations. Becoming an active participant in the construction of meaning for the incarcerated while concurrently searching for ways to bring about social justice very often requires an engagement with narrative methods. Reflexivity in using the processes of storytelling – the co-construction of life histories through chronicling and active listening techniques – is essential to uncovering a wealth of untapped data through narrative, particularly in a field as physically, emotionally and methodologically limiting as prison (Schlosser, 2008).

It is an important project, as researchers, for us to move our findings beyond the localized temporal and spatial constraints of our particular empirical cases. Our data are housed in fixed arenas of social life; they provide us with a cross-section of a moment and location and allow us to take a look behind the curtain, temporarily and at limited angles. We are restricted by the constraints of time and place and we can never go back and peek behind the same curtain twice. So, the limitedness of the availability of our data requires us to go further than those empirical moments and connect what we have been privileged enough to see to the ways in which the same mechanisms operate in other social arenas and behind all sorts of other curtains. Indeed, it is our privilege and responsibility not just to report what we see but also to use our knowledge and resources to effect positive change.

Science is no longer (nor has it ever really been) value-free. Our participants are human beings whose subjectivity should be as important to us as it surely is to them. Our responsibility, then, is to offer solutions when our research reveals that their well-being is threatened. In the course of doing criminological research we see where threats to individual liberties, freedoms and basic human rights abound. The sociology of prisons, in particular, is wrought with opportunities to witness how the individuals we come to know and, sometimes even understand, are entrenched in the institutional failings of a broken system (Schlosser, 2013).

The task of connecting a postmodern phenomenon like discursive discipline to real-world, empirical cases is made much easier when we treat modern social institutions as texts themselves. This practice allows us to read those institutions in ways that highlight subversive, controlling and seemingly natural forms of individual domination. In our reading of social institutions such as prisons as postmodern texts, we see illuminated all the ways in which these institutions are used to engage in a larger, broader and more pervasive project wherein they become the bearers of the production of social reality (Henry & Milovanovic, 1996). Reality is defined and constructed for us every day through the drafting of common meta-narratives. Institutions such as prisons, correctional systems, schools, financial institutions, houses of political import, medical arenas, classrooms and courtrooms act merely as the laborers, building social constructions of reality in highly efficient, standardized ways. However, institutions themselves are not the owners of these realities and narratives, they are simply the workers on the factory floor, producing and reproducing a hegemony that the rest of us are compelled to consume and, eventually, reproduce ourselves.

Stuart Henry and Dragan Milovanovic (1996) provide a clear explanation of the processes of construction and the subsequent reconstitution of social reality just described:

> Once social structures are constituted as summary representations, their ongoing existence depends upon their continued and often unwitting reconstruction in everyday discourse, a discourse replete with tacit understandings whose basis lies outside the realm of intrinsic intersubjective communication and intersubjectively established meaning. Core meaning constructs are typically pre-constructed elsewhere as part of our common 'stock of knowledge' (68).

In institutions of criminal justice, the discourse of personal responsibility, self-blame and rational choice imputed onto the inmates housed there come from those "core meanings," which, in fact, *are* invented elsewhere; pre-fabricated and delivered wholesale, straight to the prisons. These institutions of punishment then act as middlemen, disseminating the dominant discourses of American culture through the media of legitimacy and the notion that they are naturally constituted ways of acceptable living and thinking. However, the question then becomes: who, if not the institutions themselves, are the authors of the dominant discourses? The answer is not as complicated as it might seem.

References

Becker, H. S. (1963). *The outsiders: Studies in the sociology of deviance.* New York: The Free Press.

Benaquisto, L. & Freed, P. J. (1996). The myth of inmate lawlessness: The perceived contradiction between self and order in inmates' support for criminal justice sanctioning norms. *Law and Society Review, 30*(3), 481–512.

Bosworth, M. (2007). Creating responsible prisoners: Federal admission and orientation packs. *Punishment and Society, 9*(67), 67–85.

Bourdieu, P. (1977). *Outline of a theory of practice.* Cambridge: Cambridge University Press.

Bruner, J. (1991). The narrative construction of reality. *Critical Inquiry, 18*(1), 1–21.

Crites, S. (1971). The narrative quality of experience. *Journal of the American Academy of Religion, 39*(3), 291–311

Denzin, N. K. (2001). *Interpretive interactionism.* Thousand Oaks, CA: Sage Publications.

Faith, K. & Near, A. (2006). *13 Women: Parables from prison.* Vancouver, BC: Douglas & McIntyer.
Foucault, M. (1979). *Discipline and punish: The birth of the prison*. New York: Second Vintage Books.
Fox, K. J. (1999a). Changing violent minds: Discursive correction and resistance in the cognitive treatment of violent offenders in prison. *Social Problems, 46*(1), 88–103.
—— (1999b). Reproducing criminal types: Cognitive treatment for violent offenders in prison. *The Sociological Quarterly, 40*(3), 435–53.
Goffman, E. (1963). *Stigma: Notes on the management of spoiled identity.* New York: Simon and Schuster.
Gubrium, J. & Holstein, J. (1998). Narrative practice and the coherence of personal stories. *The Sociological Quarterly, 39*(1), 163–87.
Gudmundsdottir, S. (1996). The teller, the tale and the one being told: The narrative nature of the research interview. *Curriculum Inquiry, 26*(3), 293–306.
Henry, S. & Milovanovic, D. (1996). *Constitutive criminology: Beyond postmodernism*. Thousand Oaks, CA: Sage Publications.
Johnson, P. C. (2003). *Inner Lives: Voices of African American Women in Prison*. New York: NYU Press.
Lemert, E. M. (1951). *Social pathology.* New York: McGraw-Hill.
Liebling, A. (1999). Doing research in prison: Breaking the silence? *Theoretical Criminology, 3*(2), 147–73.
McKendy, J. P. (2006). 'I'm very careful about that': Narrative and agency of men in prison. *Discourse and Society, 17*, 473–502.
Maines, D. R. (2000). The social construction of meaning. *Contemporary Sociology, 29*(4), 577–84.
Maruna, S. (2008). *Making good: How ex-convicts reform and rebuild their lives.* Washington, DC, American Psychological Association.
Matza, D. (1969). *Becoming deviant*. Englewood Cliffs, NJ: Prentice-Hall.
Medlicott, D. (2001). *Surviving the Prison Place: Narratives of Suicidal Prisoners.* Aldershot, UK: Ashgate.
Paik, L. (2006). Are you truly a recovering dope fiend? Local interpretive practices at a therapeutic community drug treatment program. *Symbolic Interaction, 29*(2), 213.
Polkinghorne, D. E. (1996). Explorations of narrative identity. *Psychological Inquiry, 7*(4), 363–7.
Presser, L. (2008). *Been a heavy life: Stories of violent men*. Chicago: University of Illinois Press.
Reiman, J. (2009). The moral ambivalence of crime in an unjust society. In J. Reiman and P. Leighton (Eds.), *The rich get richer and the poor get prison: A reader.* New York: Pearson.
Schlosser, J. (2008). Issues in interviewing inmates: Navigating the methodological landmines of prison research. *Qualitative Inquiry, 14*(8), 1500–525.
—— (2013). Bourdieu and Foucault: A conceptual integration toward an empirical sociology of prisons. *Critical Criminology, 21*(1), 31–46.
Smith, D. (1999). *Writing the social: Critique, theory and investigations.* Toronto, ON: The University of Toronto Press.
Somers, M. (1994). The narrative constitution of identity: A relational and network approach. *Theory and Society, 23*(5), 605–49.

Sorensen, R. C. (1950). Interviewing prison inmates. *Journal of Criminal Law and Criminology, 41*(2), 180–2.

Sykes, G. (1958). *The society of captives: A study of a maximum security prison*. Princeton, NJ: Princeton University Press.

Thoits, P. (1995). Identity-relevant events and psychological symptoms: A cautionary tale. *Journal of Health and Social Behavior, 36*(1), 72–82.

4 The architects

"I coulda changed – I chose to live this life. Maybe it's 'cause I wasn't trying to break the cycle."

Sam, 20

Expert knowledge

Expert knowledge is the basis for the institutional meta-narrative and the medium through which discursive discipline is enacted. It is the overarching program imposed upon wards of the state, expressed through layers of political discourse and touted as definitive. It is comprised of the tools and resources used by policy makers, administrators, practitioners and scholars to inform policies and programs. Expert knowledge takes a definable form when it is used as the basis for the construction of mandatory prison classes like the one discussed here.

In prison, expert knowledge is played out through the relationships among staff and inmates via the dictates of policy. It is the discourse that relays what behaviors and attitudes are right or wrong, good or bad, valuable or wasteful. It is the moral authority that guides and shapes the discursive landscape of the prison. Expert knowledge is the voice of higher loyalties, commanding not only attention and respect but also acceptance and submission. To the inmates, the 'experts' writing the discourses of prison life are faceless, nameless, disembodied 'others' reigning over and managing even the most minute details of their lives. Expert knowledge is Bourdieu's (1977) "social orchestration without a conductor"; his "socially constituted system of cognitive and motivating structures, and the socially structured situation in which the agents' *interests* are defined, and with them the objective functions and subjective motivations of their practices" (76).

Expert knowledge is the 'habitus' of the disciplinary life of prisons. It is Foucault's (1979):

> multiplicity of often minor processes, of different origin and scattered location, which overlap, repeat, or imitate one another, support one

> another, distinguish themselves from one another according to their domain of application, converge and gradually produce the blueprint of a general method (138).

Expert knowledge is the unquestioned way of life that orders, controls and dominates prison inmates (and, indeed, the rest of us). It demands the inmates' total involvement and, in doing so, engages them as participants in the reproduction of their own domination. The less compelled they are to question the information and policies being enacted upon them by these "experts," the more they manage to reproduce the self-alienating structures of disciplinary life.

For prison inmates, the imposition of expert knowledge comes from multiple levels of authority. The state Department of Corrections hands down policy decisions and the staff at individual prisons are held with the charge of carrying them out. So, the experts doling out knowledge to inmates in prison are politicians (nationally and locally), Departments of Correction administrative staff, prison staff, writers of policy, creators of in-prison programs, directors of reentry initiatives, prison guards, professional scholars called upon for their opinions and taxpayers. However, these experts rarely make physical appearances in prison and never explain the reasoning behind or motivations for the policies they implement to those whom they expect to follow along.

Departments of Correction function to serve the needs and demands of the citizenry. As a result, a Department of Corrections may operate by basing its policies on the interests of a temperamental clientele: the taxpaying public. In fact, expert knowledge is truly the reiteration of the dominant discourses in contemporary American politics. What the people want is to feel validated in the idea that their hard work and individual accomplishments are valuable. In order to feel that validation, it is essential to separate those who work for their rewards from those who make excuses for their failures. In constructing acceptable ways of speaking about one's successes, the essential cultural vocabulary includes personal responsibility, hard work and independence. It is no surprise, then, that in the act of separating "us" from "them," convicted criminals are seen as the group severely lacking in the values and morals of everyday American entrepreneurs. As a result, politicians vying for reelection and policy makers interested in obtaining tax dollars have an interest in producing expert knowledge that aligns with the demands of the contemporary cultural landscape, not the least of which involves using common languages, dialogues and vocabularies to construct one master meta-narrative.

While the Department of Corrections acts as a service provider for the citizens of the state, the political pressures can contribute to the adoption of policies and programs not fully tested or researched. The result can lead to the implementation of programs within prisons that lack oversight, assessment or practical application. The Department of Corrections deals in an expertise that involves the incarceration, management, custody, care and release of convicted criminals. Its expert knowledge, however, often does not extend to dealing with the realities of life behind bars, the pressures of the world beyond release, the individual mental-health needs of inmates or their successful reentry back into the community. Due to immense pressure from taxpayers, Departments of Correction may bring in outside sources of expert knowledge in order to address some of the issues they are not equipped to handle. Sometimes, the adoption of programs and policies touted to "reduce recidivism" are poorly constructed, improperly implemented and dangerously objective. The following section outlines the particular case of the Missouri Department of Corrections in its quest to enact discursive discipline through the use of expert knowledge and the changes it implemented, which spanned the better part of a decade.

Department of Corrections

According to the most recent data available, as of December, 2013, census data from all adult facilities under the direction of the Missouri Department of Corrections indicated 31,537 offenders were currently housed in correctional institutions. Of those prisoners, 16,589 were convicted of violent crimes, 6,918 were convicted of property crimes, 5,587 were convicted of drug crimes, 1,205 were convicted of driving while intoxicated and 1,238 were convicted of other types of crimes (Missouri Department of Corrections, 2013). The Missouri Department of Corrections (2009a, 1) holds to the following mission statement:

> The Department of Corrections with victims, communities and state and local governments improves public safety through secure confinement and effective community interventions.
>
> Through our cooperative efforts to provide effective correctional services, we hold offenders accountable for their behavior and prepare them to be productive citizens.

In constructing the range of language required to fully compile a cache of expert knowledge, the Department of Corrections takes a strong position on the role of the inmates in its charge. The expert narrative constructed begins with the ideological standpoint that "offenders are accountable for their behavior" and likewise implies that, due to their incarceration they are not currently, nor were they previously, "productive citizens." In this way, all inmates are drawn together as a group of previously unaccountable and currently unproductive people. This initial categorization is essential to the production of a strong expert knowledge base grounded solidly in the ideological demands and contemporary visions of the place of subjectivity and individual action in the larger cultural matrix. In other words, holding inmates accountable and making them productive are goals that allow the Department of

Corrections to align its political agenda with the requirements for responsible living popular in our larger cultural constructions (Henry & Milovanovic, 1996). In making this move to align itself with the demands of the populace, the Department of Corrections is able to expand and strengthen its base of expert knowledge exponentially by weaving it into pre-existing cultural definitions and expectations of subjectivity. Now, the questioning of or resistance to policy by inmates can not only be characterized by the institution as insubordinate and uncooperative, but also as wholly un-American.

The Department of Corrections' move to further align itself with the demands of the public began in 2002 when the state of Missouri implemented a new initiative that called for serious changes in the way the corrections system was managed and how it handled the transition of inmates from prisons back into the community. The initiative, called the Missouri Reentry Process, was pioneered by Republican Governor Matt Blunt when he took office in 2005. The Missouri Reentry Process adheres to the following tenets:

a. Offenders can change and be productive citizens.
b. The Missouri Reentry Process begins when an offender enters the Department of Corrections.
c. The Missouri Reentry Process is a responsibility, which is shared by the offenders, their families, community agencies and the state.
d. A seamless continuum of services should be in place for each offender leaving the institution to reduce future criminal behavior.
e. Offenders should receive training, education and treatment to better prepare them for transition to the community.
f. Offenders who are better prepared to fulfill their obligations to their children can reduce the intergenerational cycle of crime.
g. Employment that provides adequate income is critical to the offender's financial stability in the community.
h. Stable housing is one key component, which impacts the stability of the offender in the community.
i. Faith-based support can play an important part in an offender's reentry to the community.
j. Offenders should leave the institution as healthy as possible and have access to healthcare in the community.
k. Victims must be allowed to participate in the Missouri Reentry Process and be supported by it.

(Missouri Department of Corrections, 2006)

At the beginning of Governor Blunt's term in 2005, the Missouri Reentry Process published a guide to the initiative titled *Missouri Makes Its Move*. The publication, intended for both the public and practitioners in the field of corrections in Missouri, sought to explain the process in plain language. It presented statistics illustrating the need for other departments and community organizations to partner with the Missouri Reentry Process to provide services for inmates upon release. One of the key facets of the publication was to explain what the Department of Corrections would do differently and how the Reentry Process would work. The following excerpt from the publication explains the goals of the Reentry Process:

> *Is this just another program to coddle criminals?* This partnership will hold offenders responsible for their behavior and accountable for their actions from the day they enter prison through release and community supervision. Through the combined efforts of the participating agencies, an offender is required to develop a transition accountability plan to accomplish what is needed to succeed upon release. There are sanctions for those who fail to follow their plans. This partnership also seeks to break the inter-generational cycle of incarceration among offender mothers, fathers and their children.
>
> (Missouri Department of Corrections, 2005)

The alignment of the state's agenda with the expectations and demands of the public is most evident here. This section of the publication is organized as if in direct response to a hypothetical question that the Department of Corrections anticipated being asked. In a blatant effort to stave off what it anticipates as a skeptical public; the state preempts its potential critics by presuming to answer their potential concerns up front. In its description of the Missouri Reentry Process, the state anticipates that the public will ask: "is this just another program to coddle criminals?" The assumption is that the public (the audience for this publication) already assumes that there are too many programs instituted in prisons designed to "coddle" criminals. In order to align itself with the "tough on crime" stance prevalent in the contemporary political landscape, the Missouri Department of Corrections makes efforts to assure the taxpayers that the Missouri Reentry Process is, in fact, in line with a punitive model of criminal justice. So, despite prior statements in the same publication that acknowledge the need for community-based partnerships in ensuring the successful reentry of the offender, the Missouri Department of Corrections here, in its anticipatory response to potential critics, places the responsibility for successful community reentry solidly on the inmates. In fact, it states definitively that inmates who do not take responsibility will face sanctions. The implication (and reality) here is that the "sanctions" they face for non-compliance include future or extended incarceration.

Following the brainstorming phase of the Missouri Reentry Process, the Department of Corrections came out with its *Strategic Plan* documenting the goals of the process from its beginning in 2005 to its anticipated completion in 2009. The following are excerpts from the *strategic plan* indicating the implementation of cognitive self-change philosophies:

> *Probationers and Parolees:* Utilize 'Pathway to Change' program to improve motivation to obtain and maintain employment with selected offenders (4).

Functional Context Education: Curricula integration among academic, career and technical and life skills education in Department of Corrections institutions. The ultimate goal is to produce an "employable offender." All areas of education must overlap and share, teaching functional concepts. Measure student progress through: completion of education components, attainment of employment upon release, earnings level of that employment, and job retention (5).

Customer Service: Ensuring Public Safety: Establish standardized cognitive skills development curriculum for use in both institutional and community supervision (7).

Accountability, Budget and Personnel: Consolidate, reduce or eliminate programs without affecting the level of service (11).

(Missouri Department of Corrections, 2009a)

It is important to note that the Missouri Department of Corrections states that the purpose of instituting the 'Pathway to Change' program in its prisons is to "improve motivation to obtain and maintain employment" and that "the ultimate goal is to produce an 'employable offender.'" It stands to bear, then, that in the further alignment of its goals, the Missouri Department of Corrections believes that offender employability is a central component to maintaining the support of the public. Again, these statements fit well within the acceptable cultural discourses emphasizing hard work and personal responsibility. Further, in using phrases such as "customer service," the Department of Corrections further writes the meta-narrative with language common in economic and financial realms. Using the language of our capitalistic service economy, the Department of Corrections fashions itself as a service provider for clients and customers. In using this business-model type of narrative to define its own role, the Department of Corrections becomes situated as an independent industry, a company that operates to satisfy its customer base by supplying the public with what it demands: public safety through creating rational and responsible prison inmates.

As a supplement to the *Strategic Plan*, the Department of Corrections also constructed a chart called "MRP History Results and Future Plans," documenting the progress of the Missouri Reentry Process (MRP) over the years. Although the chart is absent of dates, the following excerpt indicates the state of cognitive self-change philosophies historically throughout the process:

Before MRP: Lacked a department wide cognitive skills program.

Result of MRP: Contracted service, 'Pathway to Change', an evidence-based cognitive skills program, designed to help the offender understand their thoughts, decision-making habits and alter their behaviors.

Future Plans: Expansion to all institutions, probation and parole offices and institutional treatment centers, completed (4) (Missouri Department of Corrections, 2009a).

Finally, as evidence of the success of the Missouri Reentry Process, the Department of Corrections (2009b) published on its website two *Success Stories* about inmates who had benefited from the efforts of the Reentry Process.

1. An offender at XXX Correction Center writes:

   I'm currently housed in 2B, and was very reluctant to come here, knowing with my early release of 33 days out, I would not have much, if any use, for a Transitional Housing Unit [THU].

   I must say that I was wrong about the THU. Since my move here I've gotten my resume, cover letter and letter of explanation typed. I've had classes pertaining to housing, financial assistance, child support and others. Although this doesn't pertain to my situation, it was very informational to someone whom might not be versed in life enough to know where to begin.

   The staff in the THU made themselves readily available for assistance in anyway possible. I've gotten several job leads for New Mexico and feel the ladies gave me their complete attention and assistance. I only hope other inmates here will take advantage of this very organized department on the facility.

   Thanks [sic] you and all the ladies in the THU for this program. It is much appreciated (Missouri Reentry Process Success Story, 2/19/2008).

2. Donnie was released on 11/29/07 and engaged with Connections to Success on 12/03/2007.

   Donnie's teeth were pulled while he was incarcerated. Before we were able to successfully send him out on job search, we knew that he had to get dentures. One of our … Resource Managers contacted a dentist from her congregation who provided his services pro bono to Donnie. The dentist came in as early as 6:30 for multiple days to work with Donnie before his other patients arrived. This is the true power of working within our communities to provide services and resources to the men and women that are determined to move forward. Donnie is now ready to seriously begin job searching and his confidence has soared!

   We were also able to provide him with a new winter coat, thanks to a generous donation from one of our employer/partners!! [emphasis in original] (Missouri Reentry Process Success Story, 1/8/2008).

To conclude its rationale for engaging in the Reentry Process, the state of Missouri used two "success" stories as a way to punctuate the utility of the program. In referencing its successes, the Department of Corrections referenced two individuals whom it believed had received benefits from their participation in the program. In using these "real life" accounts as a testament to the success of the program, the Department of Corrections further validated its efforts and provided specific, local and anecdotal evidence of the program's success as a way to satiate the general public. The evidence of the program's success, however, is neither verifiable nor reliable based on the data provided from the two cases. What these success stories do, however, is drive the meta-narrative to a tidy and believable conclusion; thus further emphasizing the unquestionable authority of expert knowledge.

It is evident that during multiple stages of the implementation of the Missouri Reentry Process, the Department of Corrections maintained a commitment to engaging cognitive self-change philosophies and strategies throughout its institutions. The 'Pathway to Change' program was obtained through a contract with a Utah-based company (Clime International) to "improve motivation to obtain and maintain employment with selected offenders." Further, the Missouri Department of Corrections (2010) stated that:

> Pathway to Change is an essential element of the client management approach utilized by the Missouri Department of Corrections. Research shows that building cognitive skills has been the single most effective intervention technique that can be employed by corrections. The curriculum adopted by the Department will address issues related to criminal behavior and recidivates such as: factors that lead to criminal behavior, responsible decision making, examination of values and attitudes, successful relationships, identifying and correcting thinking errors. This is a twelve-week program. The first 6 sessions must be completed in chronological order and the last 6 may be completed as chosen by the client/offender.

It was necessary for the Missouri Department of Corrections to look outside its home offices for help in achieving its goal of helping offenders find employment. It is unclear how the Missouri Department of Corrections identified and decided upon 'Pathway to Change' as the program to use, however, its adoption effectively introduced cognitive self-change therapies into Missouri prisons. In doing so, the Department of Corrections was able to link the new program to its other goals, which include holding "offenders responsible for their behavior and accountable for their actions from the day they enter prison through release and community supervision." The Department of Corrections was able to contract out expert knowledge and universally apply the program philosophies to inmates near release while simultaneously upholding its primary principle of creating an employable and, above all, responsible offender.

Given the prevalence of criminological and psychological data supporting cognitive-behavioral prison programs, it is not surprising that the Missouri Department of Corrections chose to implement 'Pathway to Change.' While the documentation regarding why the DOC chose this particular program is murky, a closer look at the experiences of inmates participating in the program is warranted. Statistical and other quantitative data seem to indicate that properly designed CBPs can reduce the risk of recidivism, but no studies have yet investigated the qualitative effects of such programs on the experiences of the inmates themselves. The comparative analysis presented here examines prison inmates' discursive representations of their most personally relevant life experiences and juxtaposes those stories with the content of the 'Pathway to Change' lesson manual and the expected outcomes of the Department of Corrections. The data analyzed take into account the program material indicating what the inmates *should* say as well as the interview material representing what they *did* say. The result is a discursive struggle that finds its tension played out in some very real ways.

References

Bourdieu, P. (1977). *Outline of a theory of practice.* Cambridge: Cambridge University Press.

Foucault, M. (1979). *Discipline and punish: The birth of the prison.* New York: Second Vintage Books.

Henry, S. & Milovanovic, D. (1996). *Constitutive criminology: Beyond postmodernism.* Thousand Oaks, CA: Sage Publications.

Missouri Department of Corrections. (2005). *Missouri makes its move.* Available online at http://doc.mo.gov/mrp/mrp.php.

—— (2006). *Missouri reentry process principles.* Available online at http://doc.mo.gov/mrp/mrp.php.

—— (2009a). *Strategic plan.* Available online at http://doc.mo.gov/mrp/mrp.php.

—— (2009b). *Success stories.* Available online at http://doc.mo.gov/mrp/mrp.php.

—— (2010). *Supervision strategies and treatment alternatives.* Available online at http://doc.mo.gov.

—— (2013). *Annual report.* Available online at http://doc.mo.gov.

5 The site

> "There's only one way – you gotta be civilized."
>
> Alex, 22

The narratives: expert knowledge as cognitive self-change

'Pathway to Change': cognitive self-change

In the state of Missouri in 2009, the Department of Corrections mandated that certain prisons participating in the newly established "Missouri Reentry Process" would be required to institute a cognitive-behavioral program called 'Pathway to Change.' The inmates enrolled in the class where the research for this book was conducted were men living in a Transitional Housing Unit (THU) in a medium-security prison. They were each scheduled for release from prison within one year, having served the majority of their sentences in the general population. The crimes for which they were convicted were variable, ranging from violent offenses to technical violations of parole. All the men were required (among other things) to complete the 'Pathway to Change' class to the satisfaction of prison staff before they would be cleared for release.

The data for this book come from my interviews with thirty inmates and the instructor's manual of the 'Pathway to Change' (2005) class. In order to best reference issues of recidivism, I interviewed individuals scheduled for release within one month to one year, all of whom were participating in the Missouri Reentry Process. The crimes for which they were incarcerated were variable; however, the vast majority were incarcerated because of technical violations of parole or probation for an earlier charge.

One-half (fifteen) of the participants were first-time offenders and one-half (fifteen) were recidivists. *First-time offenders* are defined here as any individual currently serving a sentence at the prison who had not previously served time in an adult state correctional facility, court-mandated in-patient drug or mental health treatment facility and/or federal prison. Further, *recidivist* is defined as any individual serving time in the prison who has also served any amount of time in any or all of the aforementioned facilities, regardless of the charges incurred for the first or subsequent sentences.

My participants ranged in age from twenty-one years to forty-two years with an average age of twenty-five. Twenty of the thirty men I interviewed were fathers and twenty-one of them had dropped out of high school. Nine of my interviewees had either graduated from high school or completed their GED requirements by the time of our meeting. Eleven of my participants self-identified as Black, seventeen as White, one as Native American and one as Latino.

Staff at the prison provided me with an office in which to conduct the interviews within close proximity to but private from administrative staff and prison guards. I conducted the first fifteen interviews with the "first timers" over a one-month period, interviewing two offenders per day, three days a week. The second set of interviews was with the recidivists and involved interviews with three offenders per day, three days a week. All interviews were concluded within three months with one month off in between interview sets for transcription.

The participants were all drawn from the same THU, designed for inmates with upcoming release dates. Because they were all scheduled for release within one year, the men living in the THU were all participants in the Missouri Reentry Process and, thus, also the 'Pathway to Change' program. Each of the inmates was required to complete twelve modules of the program over twelve weeks (Missouri Department of Corrections, 2010). The men shared a large dormitory cordoned by low walls and bunk beds. They shared shower and bathroom facilities, pay phones and an outdoor recreational area. The men had meals with offenders from other parts of the prison campus in the cafeteria three times per day. Many of the offenders from the THU where I drew my sample took GED classes or were involved in a voluntary work release program.

Consent and disclosure forms for each participant were written at a sixth-grade reading level (per University Institutional Review Board specifications) and I provided each inmate with a copy of the form and read it to them so as to ensure their complete, informed consent. The interview instrument collected data including the inmates' demographics (age, education level, self-specified class, family size and makeup, hometown location, charges and circumstances for current incarceration, prior arrests/convictions, disciplinary problems in prison and expected release dates) in the form of a semi-structured interview schedule. The semi-structured interview schedule functioned primarily as a rapport-building device (Schlosser, 2008).

Narratives

The next step in the interview (in most cases) involved abandoning the instrument after it served the purpose of collecting basic demographic information and building rapport. I asked the inmates to construct a narrative of their experiences both in prison and out. This open-ended storytelling element of the interview often began after I asked them to explain the reason for their current incarceration. I found this question served as a good bridge from the basic questions I asked initially because it allowed the participants to take charge of the interview themselves and begin to tell their story.

Because the University Institutional Review Board (IRB) forbade me from tape-recording my interviews, I was restricted to taking hand-written notes as they told their stories. The manner in which the stories took form is based on the narrative method of recording "identity moments" in an interview setting (Schlosser, 2008). Identity moments are used as a technique by the interviewer wherein participants tell their stories and the interviewer guides them to recount certain moments in their life they feel helped lead to their current position. Often, identity moments emerge as a natural progression of story-telling as participants typically feel inclined to mention those events in their lives that resonate years later as being life-changing, important occurrences. Their identity, who they believe themselves to be, is tied up in the revelation of those moments in the history of their lives. Identity moments are not restricted to specific events. Often, a moment emerges from an interviewee's description of a time period in their lives that eventually culminated into a memorable and specific conclusion. An interviewer restricted to taking notes by hand can find using the technique of encouraging participants to relay identity moments very helpful in creating a timeline of significance in their lifestory. Although taking notes by hand during a narrative session is less than ideal, certain restrictions in the field are often not negotiable and researchers can learn to make the best of a difficult situation. While the potential for the narratives to be undermined by the researcher's own voice exists, using the technique of encouraging identity moments can help significantly reduce the need for the researcher to supplement too much of the story.

In my own interviews, the participants' stories always included a description of the circumstances, contexts and players involved in the events that led up to their arrest. I often used prompts and direct questions to encourage the participants to discuss their feelings and emotions while telling their stories, as they sometimes seemed reluctant to offer this information up front. Likewise, I often asked them to clarify certain statements or construct a verbal timeline of events in the story as they were often inclined to skip around or abandon one "moment" for another. After a short time, many of the participants began to tell their stories more easily and in almost every case the stories moved from the isolated narrative "moment" of the arrest for their current incarceration to involved descriptions of the events leading up to the present. More often than not, their stories went as far back as childhood and described life with their parents or caregivers and took a natural progression to stories (moments) about moving away from home, to the first time they got in trouble at school or with the police to the significant people in their lives and their current position as a prison inmate. Despite the participants' need for occasional prompts, the results of these sessions are the full narratives told by the participant and recorded by me. My interjections were infrequent and minor and were used only when necessary to encourage the flow of storytelling. Because I could not avoid using my own words during the process of writing up the stories, I acknowledge that the narratives were co-constructed by the participants and myself but contend that they were not the result of a typical interviewer/interviewee dialogic exchange.

It was my experience that most of my participants were eager to tell their stories after they felt that I was a safe person with whom to talk. Often, we went over my allotted one-hour interview time because many of the participants did not want to stop talking. Nearing the end of each interview I asked the participant future-oriented questions designed to assess their anticipated needs and goals upon release. These questions were aimed at getting a better understanding of what they believed would be necessary for them to avoid coming back to prison.

Narrative co-construction

According to Lois Presser (2009) "a narrative (or self-narrative) is sometimes referred to as a life story or life history. But a narrative is not a report on one's entire life so far. Rather, a narrative always draws selectively upon lived experience" (179). Presser emphasized that the ultimate difference between what is considered a narrative and what would be called a chronicle is the orientation of the meanings found in the act of the telling of events. In chronicles, the onus of responsibility for determining which events in the narration are important lies on the receiver of the tale, in narratives, the storyteller maintains a tighter hold on the thematic progression of the tale and what is important. Presser maintained that:

> the special utility of self-narrative for the offender: the evolution of misconduct from identifiable and culturally intelligible causes positions him/her as less bad or wrong than ascribed labels suggest (e.g., 'offender'). The 'whole story' complicates and historicizes who he/she really is (179).

My participants provided self-narratives, organized around plotted storylines of events (Agnew, 2006; Presser, 2009). The narratives in this book all begin from similar starting points and end at similar stopping points. The inmates (at my prompting) began the narrative of their path to prison in childhood and relayed to me what they saw as the specific, historically relevant events from childhood to their present incarceration. The plot, for them, was the progression of the relevant experiences that shaped their current moment of imprisonment and how they came to be who and where they are today. Their narratives also often involved detailed descriptions of other characters and how those individuals helped to develop the rest of their story. Through the process of their storytelling, certain events and people became relevant to making meaning out of who the inmates saw themselves to be and why they were in prison. These inmates were telling me the story, and making meaning for themselves, of how they came to be who they currently were: convicted criminals behind bars.

The only difference between Presser's conceptualization of offenders' interpretative narratives and mine is the analysis of meaning emergent from the inmates' words. I do not find that the inmates necessarily used narrative stories to rhetorically position themselves as morally outside of the labels given to them. In fact, the crux of my argument in this book is that their narratives reflected a deep uncertainty about the reasons for their incarceration, the events leading up to their arrests and their own roles in those events. This uncertainty, I argue, is due to the competing nature of the inmates' personal narratives and the culturally approved institutional meta-narrative pushed onto them by the state through programmatic conditioning. This position, then, brings my research closer in line with what Presser thoughtfully called a "constitutive view of narrative" (184).

Here, narrative constitutes reality in the sense that what is important is only the narrative, not what could have happened, what did happen or what will happen. The reality of the events being narrated exist within the narration, not independent of it as some touchstone of truth. The truth, for the storyteller and also for the researcher, is whatever the narrator articulates as the truth. Reality is forged here in the process of storytelling, not in the actions or behaviors that preceded the story. Taking a constitutive view of narrative construction in this way allows more freedom in the analysis of stories because we can be less concerned with people's behaviors, and give more attention to how they construct themselves in the context of those behaviors through a variety of available social, cultural and institutional discursive frames (Henry & Milovanovic, 1996).

The narratives presented here range in length from one to three typed pages. During the process of re-constructing the narratives certain themes began to emerge among the stories (Glaser & Strauss, 1967). These themes could be found, in one form or another, in each narrative and comprise the basis for the present analysis.

Institutional document analysis

Following the interviews, I analyzed documents previously collected from the Missouri Department of Corrections and the prison, including publicly accessible information as well as private documents internal to those organizations. The primary documents I collected included strategic plans, institutional goals, inmate control policies, statements of philosophy, codes of conduct for guards, prison officials and inmates generally published in handbooks and training manuals; statements of work for various prison programs and crime statistics.

The largest piece of documentary data is the instructor's manual designed to guide staff in leading the mandatory cognitive self-change class at the prison. The introductory manual, titled 'Pathway to Change,' (2005) is a forty-seven-page document that provides the group leader with twenty lessons that include everything from discussion topics and homework assignments for the inmates to cognitive restructuring exercises, positive affirmations and tools for dealing with hypothetical "real-world" encounters. 'Pathway to Change' is copyrighted by Clime International and distributed by Positive Solutions Associates. Clime International is a company that claims to develop "life skills curriculum and training resources for at-risk youth and adults in educational, criminal justice and business arenas" (Insight Learning Systems, 2009). The author of the 'Pathway to Change' manual used in Missouri prisons is Dr. George Nelson, an Associate Professor of Theater and Film at Brigham Young University and former bishop in the Mormon Church. Nelson is the president of Clime International as well as a consultant and trainer for Insight Learning Systems and various corporate "self-help" groups.

Every inmate I interviewed was required to take this class as one component to their transition out of prison as mandated by their involuntary participation in the Missouri Reentry Process. The inmates I interviewed had either already completed the 'Pathway to Change' class or were still taking it at the time of our meeting. The class met twice a week in the THU where my participants lived. A prison staff member taught the class directly from the instructor's manual after receiving six hours of "Inservice Courses" training (Missouri Department of Corrections Training Academy, 2010). The number of inmates enrolled in the class at one time was variable but they were all required to complete it and have a staff member give them a passing grade as a condition of their release. The following chapter addresses the data from both the 'Pathway to Change' program and the inmates' personal narratives by drawing out particular themes in the production and reception of expert knowledge.

Limitations of the research

Some methodological and analytical limitations are bound to occur in any research project and this endeavor is no exception. Several key issues arose and impacted my methods, which, in turn, influenced the nature of my analyses. Here, I outline these limitations and discuss their potential impact on the outcomes of this research.

First, my data on the 'Pathway to Change' class come primarily from the copy of the instructor's manual I received from a staff member at the prison. It was a second-hand reproduction with handwritten notes in the margins. I asked to keep the staff member's manual overnight to make copies, and then I returned it the next day. The other data regarding the 'Pathway to Change' class are public documents I analyzed from the Missouri Department of Corrections, particularly the Missouri Reentry Process. These documents refer to the 'Pathway to Change' program specifically, but do not go into much detail about the methods and internal structure of the class itself. Rather, the

Missouri Reentry Process refers to how 'Pathway to Change' fulfills its goals and what outcomes it expects the class to yield in response to those goals.

Having only the 'Pathway to Change' instructor's manual and the references to the class in Missouri Department of Corrections documents limited my field of usable data. I can only speak to what empirical evidence I was able to gather; however, working with what I had, my analysis of these data from the 'Pathway to Change' course allowed me to stay more closely tied to the *intended* content of the class, making it less likely that my critiques of the program are colored by institutional agents' conceptions of what the class should or could have been. In this way, my analyses are strongly grounded in the empirical data that were available to me in the highly limited field setting of the prison.

Along these lines, a second limitation to this project arose. When I first learned about the 'Pathway to Change' class the inmates were taking at the time, I had already completed several interviews. As a result, I did not ask the initial interviewees about the class specifically. At that stage in the research I made the decision not to directly ask future interviewees about the class in order to maintain consistency and continuity across my interviews. Additionally, I did not ask prison staff for their opinions about 'Pathway to Change' as they were not included as interviewees in my original research design. In fact, I never indicated to any of the participants in this study that I knew about the 'Pathway to Change' class. While this choice not to directly address the course in my interviews limits my current understanding of how the inmates believe they were affected by it, it also allows a new, almost purer analytical component to emerge. In not specifically addressing 'Pathway to Change' during my interviews, the comparative, analytic process was allowed to emerge much more organically. Qualitative codes found in both the instructor's manual and the inmates' interviews were born out of the data independently. So, the language from the manual I found in the inmates' interviews was there already rather than as a conscious response to a direct question. Likewise, the frustrations they expressed about their inability to deal with the problems they've faced in their lives and those they know await them on the outside are embedded in their narratives as an expression of their realistic concerns, rather than in direct rebuttal to a question about a class they were forced to take.

A third issue in conducting this research also arose because of my initial decision not to address the 'Pathway to Change' class directly with my interviewees or prison staff. Because of this decision, I was not able to personally observe one of these classes in action. I did not sit in on a group exercise or watch one of the lessons enacted in the prison classroom. Ultimately, this means that my data came largely from secondary, documentary sources; but again, this limitation in the available data gives way to a unique analytical position.

Similarly, I also cannot speak to the inevitable differences between policy-as-written versus policy-in-action. I mean here that because I did not observe the 'Pathway to Change' class directly, I also cannot know how closely the instructor followed the guidelines and lessons in the course manual. Based on the handwritten notes in the margins of the copy I received, it is a fairly safe assumption that for at least some of the lessons the instructor deviated from or omitted course material. Again, though, there is no way for me to know the extent of these deviations or how they influenced the inmates' participation in the course or its outcomes.

I can say, however, that the 'Pathway to Change' course was a new addition to the prison curriculum as a result of the Missouri Reentry Process and that it was required in the prison where I researched. I can speculate, then, that because it was a new program prison staff likely stuck closely to the program material at the risk of compromising the prison's position in the Missouri Reentry Process.

The limitations to the research addressed here are important points of critique. No research design, however, is perfect and in the incredibly restrictive environment of prison certain immediate decisions must be made in the field that can have unforeseeable effects on the outcomes of the overall project.

Telling stories

My aim here is to tell a story that illustrates the details and the nuances of a cognitive-based program in prison. Similar programs have traditionally been studied through meta-analyses of outcomes, rather than as the specific, particular, distinctive classes implemented on real people in actual prisons. It is important to give a face to these programs and study them on an individual basis so we can determine precisely *how* they function, rather than simply *if* they do. In taking a deeper look into the program material of these types of classes in conjunction with listening to the words and experiences of the inmates forced to take them, we can pull apart multiple layers of meaning and get closer to the heart of how these classes influence recidivism, and at what cost.

To accomplish these goals, narrative-style interviewing was a key component in this research. Due to the nature of my participants' current social position as incarcerated individuals, having been found guilty of committing a crime, inmates in prison are perhaps more eager than others to tell their stories for a number of reasons. First, the fact of their incarceration is the consequence of a set of preceding events. These preceding events, whatever they might be and whenever they might have started, are the elements of a narrative waiting to be told.

Second, it is typical in stories of involuntary incarceration for there to be two or more "sides"; at least that of the authorities and that of the inmate. The "winning" side, in these cases is always the authorities due to the fact that their side has been told and, as a result, the inmate received punishment. That there is a whole other side to the story of an individual's incarceration is a fact that is often ignored and thus lies dormant. The release of this story requires an opportunity; but such opportunities are scarce in a place where the winner makes the rules.

It seems that, given the opportunity to tell their stories, inmates in prison become the narrators of their lives in ways that bring context to the fore. The stories I heard were styled such that the contextual realities of their lives became the flesh on the bones of their existence as prisoners. Many of my participants jumped at the chance to tell someone about what had happened in their lives, their childhoods, their addictions and their incarceration. A few were reluctant and seemed unable to open up, but for the vast majority of the inmates my presence and mere interest in them seemed to work as a catalyst for their storytelling. Interestingly, the stories they told were mostly void of statements indicating blame, justifications or excuses. Certainly, there were explanations of why they behaved the way they did, but rarely did their stories accuse anyone other than themselves of wrongdoing.

For the most part I am not interested in whether the stories they told were the "truth." I am not equipped to judge the accuracy of their personal histories. Because of this position, I worked from the assumption that whatever stories they told were true for them. I am not, however, naïve; I realize that my gender, age, race, education and personal appearance likely affected how they responded to the interview questions, the language they used and which stories they chose to tell me (Schlosser, 2008). I did my best to reduce the impact of these influences by paying particular attention to everything from my personal appearance to my vocabulary. I tried to mitigate my appearance as a young, educated, White woman, but I was also honest about who I was and why I was there. Ultimately, though, I am not concerned with whether an offender "really did" commit a crime or whether, for example, a police officer planted drugs on them. My methodological and theoretical stance is that these stories constitute reality for the inmates in the context of the vocabularies and discourses available to them via their place in the prison as well as the larger cultural community. At the same time, I acknowledge the inherent subjectivity in the recounting of personal events and emphasize in my analyses those interpretations (Presser, 2009). It is neither my place nor my desire to judge the accuracy of the inmates' stories; it is simply my obligation to listen, encourage and record. In the end, whatever they believe to be the truth is good enough for me.

What follows are the co-constructed narratives of thirty inmates I spoke with in prison, presented in juxtaposition to the material in the instructor's manual of the mandatory cognitive-behavioral 'Pathway to Change' class they took. These stories represent hardened criminals, tough guys, blamers, drug addicts and slackers. However, if readers look a little closer, they'll also see innocent men, abused children, repentant fathers, hopefuls, philosophers, passionate souls and even sociologists.

References

Agnew, R. (2006). Storylines as a neglected cause of crime. *Journal of Research in Crime and Delinquency, 43*, 119–47.

Glaser, B. G. & Strauss, A. L. (1967). *The discovery of grounded theory: Strategies for qualitative research.* New York: Walter de Gruyter.

Henry, S. & Milovanovic, D. (1996). *Constitutive criminology: Beyond postmodernism.* Thousand Oaks, CA: Sage Publications.

Insight Learning Systems. (2009). *Personnel summary.* Available online at www.insightlearning.com/Home.asp.

Missouri Department of Corrections. (2010). *Supervision strategies and treatment alternatives.* Available online at http://doc.mo.gov.

Missouri Department of Corrections Training Academy. (2010). *Professional development.* Available online at http://doc.mo.gov.

'Pathway to Change'. (2005). *Introductory manual.* Clime International.

Presser, L. (2009). The narratives of offenders. *Theoretical Criminology, 13*(2), 177–200.

Schlosser, J. (2008). Issues in interviewing inmates: Navigating the methodological landmines of prison research. *Qualitative Inquiry, 14*(8), 1500–525.

6 The gap

> "This is not an experience you want. They don't treat us like we're human."
>
> David, 21

In contrast to the typical quantitative meta-analyses done in the sociological and criminological literature on "evidence based" recidivism reduction programs based primarily on cognitive-behavioral psychology, this study examines such programs in a new way. The broad-based project of discursive discipline rampant in prisons and other institutions of social and cultural control are revealed here through the in-depth analysis of one program instituted solely for the purpose of enacting discursive discipline on the inmates. This chapter, particularly, uses empirical data gathered from the program manual and inmates' individual narratives to expose the necessarily contradictory nature in the exercise of discursive discipline. The rewriting of individual experiences for the inmates by the institution is done through the medium of this 'Pathway to Change' program. It is touted by the Department of Corrections as the adhesive element binding the goals of the prison to the demands and expectations of the general public. But, as we'll see, while the program certainly aligns the prison and the public, it does so entirely at the cost of the individuals in its care.

The project of discursive discipline in this case centers on five persistent themes. What I provide next is a systematic critique of the 'Pathway to Change' class through the analysis of the empirical data gathered from the program and the inmates' narratives. Here, I examine these critiques by looking directly at the lessons laid out in the program manual and comparing them to the inmates' personal narratives.

My analyses in the following two chapters are presented thematically, addressing the following five principal critiques that characterize the prevalence of the prison's disciplinary project within the content of the 'Pathway to Change' course: self-blame, degradation, disconnection, detachment from reality and expert knowledge. This chapter looks at the first three themes, which characterize problems with the material internal to the lessons themselves. Self-blame as a discursive tactic, degradation through public shaming and the disconnection between the stated objectives of the lessons and the methods used to illustrate them are discussed here. In the next chapter, the two broader, more expansive issues unique to the 'Pathway to Change' class as a whole are discussed. Detachment from reality occurs through the media of the lessons, but it also characterizes the overall narrative of the program. The program's inability to effectively ground the lessons to any real-world problem the inmates may face characterizes this overall detachment. Additionally, the imposition of expert knowledge is further examined as it relates to the definitions provided for the inmates for abstract, philosophical ideas they may encounter in life but which become oversimplified in the program.

I explain these primary critiques by drawing directly from the language and discourse used in the body of the manual itself in comparison to the language used in the construction of the inmates' narratives. My purpose in using a comparative analysis to inform my critique is to highlight the precise ways in which the inmates are discursively disciplined through the program as the material conflicts with their narrated experiences.

My prior exposure to the inmates and the revelation of the program manual also influenced the direction and tone of the research. The themes emergent from the narratives created the framework from which I drew my critique of the program. In my pursuit of this particular analytical path, the purpose and initial questions I posed at the outset of my project changed shape and new questions became pertinent. Ultimately, I remained able to address most of my original concerns in doing this research and the inclusion of the 'Pathway to Change' and cognitive self-change program critique adds a context and depth that wasn't possible before.

Layout and content

The following is an excerpt from the introduction of 'Pathway to Change': Instructor Manual, Level I:

> Life is not just a game of chance where things happen without reason. Although things will always happen that you do not expect, you can have a huge say in your own destiny … you always have the ability to choose how you will deal with the situation.

The 'Pathway to Change' instructor's manual is set up so that an instructor would need little, if any, outside aid in following the program. The manual includes detailed, step-by-step instructions that guide the instructor seamlessly through the program. Each of the twenty lessons are prefaced by a worksheet explaining the objective, any key questions the inmates should be able to answer after completing the lesson, a list of materials the instructor will need to complete the lesson, a series of "hooks" indicating sample dialogue and instructions for preparing the class to complete the lessons on their own and a multi-step process guide including specific instructions for the teacher to lead the class in the lesson.

At the end of the manual is an appendix called "Mile Markers." A "Mile Marker" is located after each lesson in the inmates' workbook asking them to reflect on what they learned for that week's lesson. Each "Mile Marker" includes a space for the inmate to answer a prompt or question, which the instructor should provide.

Self-blame

The rhetoric of self-blame takes root in the program manual in several of the lessons. The manual takes a discursive position wherein the inmates' thoughts, feelings and ideas about their own pasts and the decisions they've made constructs a blame frame that points to the inmates themselves as the sole source of the problems in their own lives. The project of discursively disciplining the inmates begins at the outset of the program. If the inmates' answers to any of the prompts in the lessons are inconsistent with blaming themselves, they are immediately corrected and required to provide new answers until their own language adequately matches the language allowed by the program. At all times, if an inmate refuses to align his answers with the "correct" vocabulary as dictated by the program, he is reminded that insufficient participation will result in his failing the class. Failing this class, particularly, also means remaining in prison. The consequences for the inmates' failure to blame themselves and engage in the discursive restructuring of their answers and personal stories are real and severe.

Constructing the self-blame rhetoric allows the 'Pathway to Change' program to characterize the experiences of the inmates within a social and contextual vacuum, reducing the events in their lives to nothing more than bad decisions for which they alone are to blame. In the introduction to the program the theme of self-blame establishes a framework that underlies the very basis of the establishment of discursive discipline. The introduction to the program is mixed with dismissive statements that acknowledge that sometimes life events can "happen without reason" or can be the result of "circumstance," and more definitive and pointed statements like this one:

> The real truth is that most people are not willing to pay the price to get what they really want. They find it much easier to blame their problems on everyone and everything around them. You control the success or failure of this program.

This clear and unequivocal introductory statement lets the inmates know that unsuccessful people blame their problems on others, implying that successful program graduates will, instead, learn to blame themselves.

Lesson 1 ("My Life Map") further illustrates the self-blame rhetoric that runs throughout the program. Lesson 1 indicates the inmates should design a "map" to chart their progress in the class and determine where they want their lives to go in the future ('Pathway to Change', Level I, Instructor's Manual, 1–3). The instructor is guided to tell the class a hypothetical story ending in a problem where they need directions to get from the classroom to a familiar part of the prison. The inmates should create an intricately detailed map of the shortest path they could take from the classroom to the arbitrary end point. The instructor is prompted to encourage the inmates to draw a similarly detailed map, though instead of drawing out physical features, they should draw the map indicating where they want their life to go. After the inmates are finished drawing their "life maps," the manual guides the instructor to ask four questions. The manual then provides the instructor with an answer key.

The instructor is prompted to ask what the inmates have lost because of their poor choices in the past. The inmates are then instructed to identify a dollar amount they feel they have lost by their decision to commit the crime for which they are currently incarcerated. The teacher is instructed to add the total for the whole group and write it on the chalkboard.

One of the inmates I interviewed who was required to take this course was Sam, a twenty-year-old Black man from the inner city of a large metropolitan area. Sam said his first encounter with drugs was at birth when he was born to a crack-addicted mother. Everyone around him had done drugs for as long as he could remember. The first time Sam tried drugs, he was eight years old and his father got him high on marijuana. Sam has one daughter who is two years old. He currently has two brothers, five cousins and two uncles in prison, one of whom is serving a life sentence for murder.

When he was fifteen, Sam was sent to a juvenile detention center for three years because he stole a police car and hit an officer with it. When I asked Sam why he was committing crimes at such a young age he replied: "seeing everybody I grew up around was doing wrong. I don't know nothing different – as you can see, all my family here [in prison]."

After his release from the juvenile center, Sam returned home and continued to engage in illegal activity. One day, however, he and some family members were being questioned by the police for recent crimes committed in the neighborhood. During the questioning, things got out of hand and turned violent. Sam recalled: "the police shot my cousin, dead, in my mom's front yard." After witnessing the death of his cousin, Sam stole another police car and was arrested and sentenced to prison. He has served one year and three months.

I asked Sam why he thought he ended up in prison and he replied: "maybe if I'd had more discipline I might not of did some of this stuff." When I asked him whose fault it was that he was in prison he said: "I coulda changed – I chose to live this life. Maybe it's 'cause I wasn't trying to break the cycle." I asked if prison had changed him and he said: "coming here didn't make me want to change nothing. My daughter did that."

I questioned Sam about what he thought would help keep people like himself from going to prison. He replied: "a new setting. You gotta get yourself a better environment." He also said young people like himself would "have to hear it from an older person in prison." Sam also added that "females who they don't know" would have a greater influence on helping to get through to other offenders. He said: "people like you – females, authority figures who are women will keep you out." Sam believes this will be his only time in prison.

It's clear from Sam's story that he remains torn between reiterating the rhetoric of the prison institution ("breaking the cycle") by admitting blame, and reconciling some of the key, identity moments in his life over which he had little control but greatly contributed to his arrests. Sam's story was a common one in my research. His competing narratives, that of blame and responsibility and that of the detrimental influence of others, were present in almost every narrative I gathered. The inmates seemed to know what they were supposed to say, but most of them were unable to take full blame for their situations without also qualifying the contexts of their lives by introducing other characters or uncontrollable situations. For Sam, "breaking the cycle" of crime in a family where ten of the men are currently serving prison time seems wholly unrealistic. And, although Sam stated that he "coulda changed" and that, perhaps, he wasn't trying hard enough to do so, in the next breath he also said that in order to avoid prison, people like himself need a "new setting … a better environment."

The theme of self-blame in the 'Pathway to Change' course occurs prominently in Lesson 11 (23–5). The stated objective of the lesson is "to help participants understand that mistakes are an important aspect of human development." In principle, this seems like a fine lesson for anyone to learn; however, the teaching methods in the lesson leave much to be desired. The instructor is prompted to break the class into small groups where they will work together to decide which member of the group has made the most embarrassing mistake. They are to present the story to class and the other participants should vote on the funniest story, after which the "winner" should "role-play" an effective way to deal with the mistake. Similarly, part two of the lesson indicates that the inmates should write down three recent mistakes they made and the excuses they gave at the time as a way to "cover up what they did." The inmates are to read these aloud to the class and the instructor is supposed to point out that excuses are usually so "general and weak" that they can be used for almost any mistake.

The objective of the lesson is that inmates are to "learn" from their mistakes; however, once the inmates have effectively (and publicly) conveyed their shortcomings, the lesson ends without conclusion. The inmates are not taught how to learn from their mistakes, but rather how they are to blame for making them. We see in Robert's story that decision making, blame and responsibility are incredibly complex aspects of social life that deserve more thorough consideration.

Robert, a twenty-four-year-old Black man from a large midwestern metropolitan area is serving time in prison for violating his probation after he was caught stealing. When Robert was a young man living in his mother's house he began using and selling cocaine. He used the house to store, package and sell drugs. When Robert was twenty-one years old, his mother found out that he was selling drugs and kicked him out.

Robert moved in with his grandfather who was a neighborhood pastor. When Robert moved in, his grandfather told him that he must stop using drugs and get a job. Robert stayed clean for one year and got a job as a bill collector. Robert said he stayed clean because:

> If I didn't change I knew I'd go back to the same environment I came from. When you take drugs, you're not you anymore. What really did make me want to change was how much time I realized I had wasted.

After a year of staying off drugs, however, Robert felt like he was not making enough money at his job and began selling drugs again. He started using again soon after. When I asked Robert why he started using drugs again he said: "because my fragile, little mind couldn't handle it." Eventually, Robert began to supplement his income further by stealing from a large shopping mall in the area. Robert said he was able to become a very successful "booster" because he dressed nicely and knew how to talk to people. Robert was proud of his success as a booster and said that: "anything you do in this world you gotta put your heart into it – even stealing."

Robert, however, was caught and arrested for stealing at a mall a year ago. He claimed he was caught by mall security because of "the foolish girl I was with went into the mall – that's why I'm here." Robert said his accomplice was not as skilled at stealing as he was and her inexperience is what led to his arrest. Robert received probation for the mall incident but violated his probation when he stole a generator from an auto shop to sell on the street. When he was caught for theft again, Robert received a six-year sentence in state prison. He will serve one year in total.

When I asked Robert what he planned to do when he was released from prison he was adamant that he would not go back to drug dealing or stealing. He said: "insanity is when you keep doing the same thing and expect the same results." Robert said his goal is to continue his education and "figure out a way to keep minorities out of prison." I asked if he thought he will ever go back to prison and Robert said: "the foundation I'm building now will keep me out."

From his story, we see that Robert certainly made a number of mistakes and, indeed, had several excuses to go along with them. However, if we take a closer look at his narrative, we can also see something over which even the strongest individuals often have little control: addiction. Robert was addicted to crack cocaine and sold drugs and stolen goods to support his disease. In Lesson 11 of the 'Pathway to Change' program, Robert would certainly have passed with flying colors as he would have no trouble identifying past mistakes and the excuses he gave along with them; but, would Lesson 11 have really taught him to learn from his mistakes, or simply how to better blame himself? Lesson 11 does not teach Robert how to recognize the signs of addiction, where to seek treatment, how to engage supportive friends and family who have his best interests at heart, how to visualize a drug-free life, where to turn if he relapses, what to do with his time other than take drugs or how to fight the intense physiological and psychological symptoms of crack withdrawal. Lesson 11 does, however, let Robert and all the other inmates know that blaming themselves and their "weak" excuses is what really matters in finding the 'Pathway to Change.'

In Lesson 14, "Becoming More Responsible," the program espouses the self-blame ideology in an even more unique way (29–31). In keeping with the presumed 'excuses' theme of Lesson 11, the program asks the instructor to assign certain 'unpleasant situations' to small groups of inmates, such as being late to work, bouncing a check, burning dinner, getting fired or not passing an inspection. The inmates are to write potential excuses for these situations on the chalkboard and categorize them in one of three ways, 'someone else,' 'nobody,' 'me.' The objective, here, is to help inmates understand how to become a more responsible person.

The problem, however, is that (as in most of the lessons in the program) the possible 'unpleasant situations' the inmates are given are devoid of the necessary interactional and contextual elements required to fully reason acceptable solutions. How can one categorize getting fired as someone else's fault, nobody's fault or his own fault without first understanding the history behind the event? Without providing this information, the program implies that the correct answer to each question is for the inmates to identify the excuses they made as appropriate to the 'me' category. The lesson is a trap from the outset: if the inmates choose excuses that blame 'someone else' or 'nobody,' they will fail the exercise; however, if they only choose excuses for which they accept sole blame, they must concede that they are at fault, thus, essentially also conceding that for whatever events transpired leading them to prison, they are similarly to blame. The lesson constructs a no-win situation and sets the inmates up for failure. The dialogue in the manual constructs a word game wherein the inmates are told that they are learning about one thing (how to take responsibility) when they are actually learning how to give correct answers in order to pass the class. To successfully complete the lesson, the inmates are backed into a rhetorical corner and forced to reflect the language in the program, whether or not it actually applies.

We can identify the frustration with such a construction of blame in Aaron's story. Aaron is a twenty-three-year-old Black man from a medium-sized town in the Midwest. He said he grew up in a rough area surrounded by gang activity. Aaron said his first encounter with drugs was when he was twelve years old and he tried marijuana for the first time. He said: "everywhere I went, it was there." Since then, Aaron has used alcohol, prescription pills, cocaine and ecstasy.

Aaron said his troubles with the law began when he was thirteen years old, when he was arrested and subsequently spent the next six years of his life in and out of detention centers and prisons.

I asked Aaron what the main reason was for his incarceration and he replied: "I ain't pointing the finger at no one but myself." I asked if he believed he would ever come back to prison and he said: "I don't really think so. If it happens, then it's meant to happen. My partying days are done with, now I got responsibilities out there." I asked Aaron if he had any advice for others like himself and he said:

> Sign up for school but don't rush into it. You gotta set long-term goals. It's going to be hard – if it ain't rough it ain't right. That fast money could be somebody's last money. Most people are afraid of change – they don't want to move back to the neighborhood where they ain't nobody.

Here, Aaron both accepts and denies the blame for his situation. He recognizes that "pointing the finger" at himself is what he *should* do, yet he also acknowledges that there are environmental and cultural restrictions on his life. The point that "if it ain't rough, it ain't right" is an acceptable and, indeed, entirely natural way to view one's potential to succeed in life is a perspective that remains largely unaddressed in the program. For a class designed to change thinking patterns toward the goal of reducing the likelihood that these men will recidivate, it certainly neglects the elements in their lives with which they are most concerned; particularly, environmental challenges such as poverty, unsupportive family members and drug addiction. Aaron's defensive insistence that he is not pointing the finger (of blame) at anyone but himself illustrates how quickly the inmates recognize and respond to the discursive restructuring intended through the program. Aaron knows that to blame anyone other than himself would be characterized as a flawed or problematic thinking pattern, and that he would be corrected. He is quick to restructure the language and vocabulary he uses to describe his own life experiences so that it properly aligns with the meta-narrative espoused in the program.

For Darrell, a twenty-one-year-old White man from the "outskirts" of a mid-sized southern town, the choice/blame ideology espoused in the lessons seems to make sense. Darrell dropped out of school in the ninth grade but has since received his GED. When Darrell was four years old he first witnessed his mother smoking marijuana and tried it himself when he was nine years old. Since then, Darrell said he has tried meth, cocaine, PCP, ecstasy, prescription pills, LSD, mushrooms and marijuana. He said the only drug to which he was physically addicted was marijuana. When he was little, he wanted to be a race-car driver. Darrell has served seven months in prison on a five-year sentence.

I asked Darrell when his troubles started and he said they began when he was twelve. He was switched from a "preppy" school to a school with "laid back country folk where everyone just wanted to get fucked up." He began stealing money from his parents when he was twelve in order to buy beer. Darrell said his mom was "a hippie" and she began letting him do drugs in her home, so all his friends wanted to come over. At thirteen years old Darrell began selling marijuana and prescription pills but was caught and forced to transfer to another school. He said his previous school was "ninety percent whites, ten percent blacks. The place I transferred to was the exact opposite. It wasn't anything I was used to." At seventeen years old Darrell's mother kicked him out of the house "because she was sick of the [drug] traffic."

Darrell moved in with a friend and continued to sell drugs. In 2006, Darrell and his friend went to New Orleans for Mardi Gras and they were pulled over by the police, who found a gun and part of a marijuana joint. Darrell said they were released but a few minutes later they were pulled over by another officer. Darrell commented: "I think the first cop didn't have a good enough reason so he called another cop." They were pulled over for tailgating, the car was searched again and this time the officer found the drugs. Darrell spent four months in a jail in Baton Rouge and received probation.

After his arrest, Darrell moved back in with his mother and sold stolen goods for money. Darrell began driving with a suspended license and was pulled over by an officer for not having his headlights on. Darrell said: "I was so worried about the weed in my pocket, I forgot about the weed in the trunk." Darrell was given a court date but failed to appear and a warrant was issued for his arrest. Darrell said: "I can't run from this forever so I might as well turn myself in."

I asked Darrell if he thought he would eventually go to prison and he replied: "I think everyone knows the consequences of their actions and if they say they don't they're a liar." I asked him what his plans were after his release and he said: "I'm gonna quit smoking weed." I asked what it will take for him to stay out of prison and Darrell said: "honestly? A good girl." Finally, I asked Darrell what the main reason was for his current incarceration and he replied: "I don't blame no one but myself. I knew the consequences when I put that weed in the trunk. The worst part of it is going to be the record. I'll be a convicted felon."

Indeed, the blame rhetoric is strongest in Darrell's story. He admits that he is aware of the consequences of his actions and that he doesn't blame anyone but himself for his current incarceration. However, there is more to Darrell's story. Within the context of recounting the narrative of his life, Darrell chose to emphasize some pertinent identity moments. For Darrell, we see then that his words and his reality don't entirely match up. Indeed, he takes the blame for what he did and recognizes that the choices he made in life contributed to his incarceration, but he also acknowledges the strong influence of other characters in his story and the extenuating circumstances of life as a young man in poverty with a drug addiction. The 'Pathway to Change' program would neglect those extenuating factors in Darrell's story and insist that he focus only on the events and circumstances of his life over which he had complete control. Again, the problem here is that choices are never made in a context-free environment. There are always other environmental and personal elements to consider and the manual neglects these almost entirely.

Mike is a twenty-one-year-old White man from a rural town in the Midwest who dropped out of high school when he was in the tenth grade. Mike tried drugs for the first time at age thirteen and has since done marijuana, crack, meth and alcohol. Mike is in prison for receiving his second DWI (driving while intoxicated) charge. He received a two-year sentence, has served six months in prison and will be released in three months. Mike said he believes he is in prison because he was "just trying to fit in" and that "being around my family more would have kept me out of trouble." When I asked him why he was in prison right now he replied simply: "I put myself here."

Mike's acknowledgement that being around family would have helped keep him out of trouble and the admission that he put himself in prison illustrates the struggle of taking the blame in the face of contradictory experiences. Mike's discursive struggle involves reconciling the idea that his own choices brought him to prison, but that those choices were bound within the dictates of his available alternatives and the limitations of his support system.

Similarly for Martin, a twenty-two-year-old White man from a rural area in the Midwest, the problem of blame enters his story. Martin graduated from high school but was in juvenile detention centers from the time he was thirteen to sixteen for stealing money. Martin says he has used alcohol, marijuana, meth and cocaine.

Martin said the first time he got in trouble as an adult was when he and his wife stole twenty-two American Kennel Club registered puppies to sell illegally. Martin turned himself in and received 120 days in prison with five years' parole. As a condition of his parole, Martin could not drink or use drugs. Martin said that shortly after his release he began drinking and his mother told his parole officer that he was drinking. Martin was arrested again and sentenced to five years in prison but has served six months and will be out soon.

I asked Martin why he believed he was in prison today and he answered: "the first time was my fault, it was stupid. This time, I'm gonna have to pin it on my mom." Martin plans to go back to college and begin a career as a cage fighter. The basic reality of these stories is that there is rarely one person to blame for all of the things that can happen in the life of an individual. Certainly, there is usually the opportunity to choose certain behaviors over others, but the inability to control others' actions, let alone one's childhood environment, is neglected in the program.

Finally, the evidence that these men are torn between taking the blame and recognizing others' roles in their lives is clearest in Wayne's story. Wayne is a twenty-seven-year-old White man from a small town in the Midwest. Wayne said that he was from a "tougher part of the neighborhood" and was the "only white kid in a black neighborhood." He grew up in an abusive household where his father regularly beat his mother until she required hospitalization. Wayne received his GED in prison and plans on continuing his education someday.

Wayne's first conviction came when he was arrested for child abuse. According to Wayne, he was watching his three-year-old daughter and she would not go to bed. He "spanked her three times on the bottom and put her in the corner for fifteen minutes." The next day, Wayne said his daughter told her grandparents (Wayne's in-laws) that he had spanked her. His parents-in-law reported him to the police and Wayne was arrested on child abuse charges. Upon his release, Wayne received supervised probation with a "twenty year back up" meaning that if he violated his probation, Wayne would face up to twenty years in prison. Wayne was unclear about both the terms of his probation and the charge that sent him back to prison for this second time. He was quite reluctant to discuss his charges and, in fact, began to cry when speaking of his daughter. Wayne did say that he was currently in prison serving a five-year sentence and that he was due for release in six months.

I asked Wayne what he would do to avoid going back to prison and he replied: "I don't think there's anything I could have done to stay out. The state likes to keep their hands around your shoulders, bobbing in the pool." I asked who or what was the primary reason why he was in prison now and Wayne said: "ultimately, it was me and the choice I made, but as far as this case goes, it was my ex's family."

I asked Wayne to tell me what advice he would give to someone like himself in prison. Wayne replied:

> It's not the life – I've tried to talk to the youngsters. You gotta make your choices and take it for what it is. I've made a lot of stupid choices and I'll make a lot more but I wouldn't change anything I've done.
>
> (Schlosser, 2008).[1]

The program's deficiency in teaching the inmates "how to learn from their mistakes" could not be more clearly articulated here. Wayne is entirely torn between accepting the blame frame and the reality of the circumstances and players surrounding those choices. He acknowledges that the reason he is in prison is because of the decisions he made while simultaneously shifting the locus of blame to his ex-wife's family. It is quite evident that Wayne recognizes his own role in the story of his life, but it is also evident that he refuses to shoulder the entire burden.

Wayne's experience of abuse as a child watching his father beat his mother and the fact that he is currently incarcerated on charges of child abuse is a connection entirely lost in the standardized language of the 'Pathway to Change' program. Personal history, context, opportunity and environment are not just neglected in the program; they are constructed as excuses the men use to avoid taking the blame. From these data, however, we can see that the inmates do not shy from taking the blame; in fact in most cases they acknowledge and even welcome it. However, it is also true that the data show the men are not ready to take sole and full blame for their choices or the consequences of those choices. The refusal of the program to acknowledge the gray area, the fine balance between what 'really' happened and what 'could have' happened, points to the rewriting of individual experience as a method of cognitive control. In constructing events as static and one sided, the potential rational choices of the men are made to replace the much more realistic and fairer characterization of their lived experiences: the perfect storm of circumstance, the influence of others and personal responsibility. The 'truth' of any historical occurrence lies in the mixture of these relational parts. A story of self-blame that is devoid of these other, real, elements is nothing more than a reconstruction, approximating the inmates' lived realities, but deforming their stories and reworking them into a more palatable narrative that further propels the alignment of the institutional agenda with what the rest of society believes and wants to see reflected back.

Degradation

Drawing on Garfinkel's (1956) conception of degradation ceremonies in social institutions, we see how the 'Pathway to Change' program integrates similar themes throughout the lessons. Degradation, as a social apparatus employed by one group to lower the status character of another, rests on the principle of moral indignation. According to Garfinkel, "the paradigm of moral indignation is *public* denunciation" (421). The basic tenets of degradation as enacted publicly and involuntarily on individuals in order to denounce their identities and replace them with others deemed more socially appropriate, appear prominently in the 'Pathway to Change' program. By using degradation to further lower the statuses of the inmates, they are primed to restructure their thinking patterns in ways that invalidate their personal experiences so that they may more easily recognize the gross differences between their current selves and the general, standard version of who they ought to be. By publicly engaging in degradation, the inmates become further entrenched in the disciplinary nature of the program itself in the sense that they are made to believe that the success of the program is in their hands when, in truth, what they must do to pass the program is almost entirely out of their control.

Degradation, as a new layer of discipline designed to control and reshape the lived realities of the inmates becomes evident as the tone of the manual takes a shift in Lesson 2 ("What Are My Real Values") wherein the inmates are pushed from simply thinking about their shortcomings to acting them out (3–6). Certainly, a key component to a cognitive-behavioral model of therapy includes visualization exercises designed to gently urge a client out of his or her comfort zone so as to enable them to see their own actions in a different light. However, most cognitive-behavioral therapy sessions (even group therapies) are conducted voluntarily, under the supervision of a trained mental health professional and only after some level of safety, comfort and trust has been reached by the participants (Fox, 1999). We see the beginning of a troubling trend in Lesson 2.

The objective of the lesson is for participants to determine their learning and personality styles. To do so, the inmates take a 'Personality Styles Summary' test wherein they use a 1–4 scale system to rank themselves on a variety of personality- and attitude-based questions. After they have completed the personality test, the inmates are to group themselves by personality type according to the answers they gave on the test. Once in groups, they are to use markers and large sheets of paper to create a poster indicating what they have learned about each other and what similarities they share with other group members.

After drawing their posters, the inmates are encouraged to think up a role-playing scenario they think would convince their opposite personality group to think about how drug abuse has affected them. The instructor is prompted to have each group perform a skit to the entire class and discuss whether or not they were able to better understand something about how the other groups think. The key question for the lesson is: "what values, needs, strengths and joys do you wish you could gain from the other groups?"

Lesson 2 indicates the beginning of a hidden agenda within the program. Asking prison inmates to gather into groups, create a skit and put on a performance for the class helps to break down whatever small sense of safety they may have felt to create an even more unequal power dynamic between both the inmates themselves and the inmates and the staff. In their coercion to participate as a condition of their release from prison, the inmates are subject to the instructions of the teacher. Involuntary public performances highlighting one's own failings (like drug addiction) would, for many adults, likely conjure embarrassment, anxiety and dread. The expert knowledge included in the program, through the medium of the instructor, thus has the potential to become a dividing agent. The inmates perform together for the instructor who passes judgment on that performance. In Lesson 1, the inmates were simply asked to isolate their personal choices as the reason they are in prison; in Lesson 2 they are made to act out their shortcomings in front of an audience.

Similarly, Lesson 4 requires a measure of degradation. Here, the instructor is prompted to tell a story about an adventure. The lesson then requires the inmates to act out the parts in the story, using props. As an aside, the manual instructs the teacher to consider switching the gender of the characters. In the setting of the prison, the actions of the inmates are inherently not their own. By virtue of the oppressive power structures there, every story they tell, every answer they give and every action they make is based on coercion. The implication of coercion is omnipresent, if not at all times evident. Not only would the inmates fail to pass the course if they chose not to participate, thereby buying themselves more prison time, but they would also fail to uphold whatever necessary defenses they may have managed to build as they negotiate their daily survival. The inmates are not free, and, thus are unable to choose whether or not they want to participate; rather, they are forced to perform skits and pretend to be a different gender, should the instructor dictate. There is, perhaps, no more hyper-masculine a place than a men's prison. Forcing convicted felons to put on plays where they "switch genders" ultimately serves to humiliate and degrade them. In any case, the manual does not go on to explain the purpose of "switching genders" in the play, nor does it fully explain the potential consequences of their participation on their self-esteem or safety in prison; it simply makes a blanket suggestion and leaves it up to the instructor to decide whether or not to follow through. In this case, the copy of the instructor's manual I received had a circled "X" hand-drawn next to the lesson. I take this to mean that the instructor chose not to include the performance aspect of the lesson in his/her class, although I cannot be certain.

Few of the inmates I interviewed spoke openly about the horrors of prison that most of us in the general public choose to ignore or find too upsetting to believe. Darin, however, openly admitted that his experiences in the prison environment were enough to prevent him from doing anything that could send him back.

Darin is a twenty-six-year-old White father of one. He dropped out of high school in the eleventh grade and plans on continuing his education in vocational school. Darin is in prison because he violated his probation after tampering with a motor vehicle. He has been on probation for most of his life, but this is his first time in prison.

At seventeen, Darin stole a car with a friend, used the car to turn over some vending machines, stole $400 from the machines and used it to purchase methamphetamine. Darin and his friend abandoned the car in a park but "people started opening their mouths, trying to pass the buck to us." The police questioned Darin while he was high on meth. Darin said of the questioning: "I don't know if you've ever been interrogated, but they ask you the same question about fifteen times in a row." Darin received more probation for tampering with a motor vehicle and stayed out of trouble for three years. He was arrested, however, when he was pulled over and caught with an open container of alcohol in his car. Darin received five more years of supervised probation and claims that "they wanted to wait till I was an adult and see if they could pile any more charges on."

When Darin missed two appointments in a row with his probation officer, she put out a warrant for his arrest and Darin went on the run for three years. He was eventually caught for having expired tags and sentenced to five years in prison. Darin has served nine months so far. When I asked him why he thought he was in prison, Darin answered: "my one mistake has kept me down for so long; my own mistakes got me here." I asked if he thought he would ever be back in prison he replied: "probation is a joke, period. It's a dance but prison scared the shit out of me, I've got too much out there [to go back to]." Finally, Darin said the best way to keep other young people from going to prison is to "scare the young kids. Let them have a taste of the life in here." As for himself, Darin said: "I'm done running – I got gray hairs."

For Darin, the experience of living in prison was eye opening. His suggestion for keeping young people out of prison was to scare them with the realities behind bars. So, activities like those in Lesson 4, which force the inmates to perform a skit where they act like the opposite gender (presumably effeminate) to an audience of fellow inmates and prison guards seems only to further marginalize them and, in fact, could even put them directly in harm's way. Darin's suggestion of letting the young kids "have a taste of the life in here" as a deterrent measure indicates the intensity he feels for the undesirable conditions of prison life. Not only does the program neglect this important aspect of social life in prison, but it also seems to add insult to injury by opening up further sites of embarrassment and degradation.

Nowhere in the program manual is the acknowledgment of the violence, hyper-masculinity, drug use and fear that pervades the everyday lives of prison inmates. The program never addresses the real and unspeakable acts of abuse many of the inmates are subjected to daily inside prison. There is no lesson included in the manual that teaches the inmates how to avoid being raped or beaten or how to protect themselves from other inmates or guards while they sleep or bathe. And yet, through my talks with the guards and administrators during this research, I learned that rapes and beatings happen in their prison every day. Though the guards seemed mildly concerned, they indicated that there was not much they could do to prevent what they considered to be the inevitable consequences of life in prison. Given the intensity and prevalence of violence, mandatory submission to the rules and complete lack of agency in prison, the requirement that the inmates participate in degrading and intentionally humiliating activities is compelling evidence of the disciplinary nature of such programs. By further breaking down their sense of self and the defenses they built for protection, the program effectively utilizes degradation to produce a more docile and better controlled population of inmates.

The theme of degradation as a disciplinary tactic continues in Lesson 16, titled "Your Hot Buttons" (35–6). The instructor is told to continue the role-playing theme by breaking the class up into small groups where they are to create lists of things others do that make them feel crazy. Then, they must pick the most humorous example from the list and act it out for the other inmates. Similarly, in Lesson 17 (37–9) the inmates are to be blindfolded and forced to "feel" small parts of everyday objects in front of the class until they are able to guess the object. The objective here is, apparently, to focus on the fact that people have different points of view. Finally, in Lesson 18 (39–40) the inmates must play the 'Telephone Game' to improve their communication skills. In one version, the inmates must whisper a story into another inmate's ear, who then passes the story along to someone else. The last person to hear the message must relay it aloud. The apparent objective is to illustrate that the inmates need to improve their ability to communicate. The suggested story the inmates should tell one another and repeat aloud begins:

> Patty's grandmother lives in Pittsburgh. One day she sent Patty out for pumpernickel bread for peanut butter sandwiches at Mr. Paul's store. On the way to the store, Patty met Pete. Patty and Pete went to play pinball.

Following her pinball excursion with Pete, Patty realizes she is late retrieving the pumpernickel bread from Mr. Paul's store on Prince Street. Upon returning home she discovers, to her utter dismay, that she purchased pita bread instead of pumpernickel. After reading these lessons it is not surprising that during my interviews with the inmates one of the most common themes in their stories was the search for respect in prison.

Consider David, a twenty-one-year-old Black male currently serving time in the Missouri Department of Corrections. David is from the inner city of a large midwestern urban area. He classifies his living situation growing up and into adulthood as poor and said he came from a rough neighborhood. David said he knew of up to twenty friends and family members who are also in prison. David was convicted of tampering with a motor vehicle, resisting arrest and burglary. He was high on PCP and embalming fluid at the time of his arrest.

David's first experience with drugs was when he was five years old, when he saw his grandfather doing cocaine. Since that experience, David has done marijuana and the hallucinogen PCP. When David was fourteen years old his grandfather gave him a pistol and said: "you'll never be broke if you have this," so David began using the gun to rob homes, used-car lots and pedestrians on the street. David was caught numerous times for various misdemeanors but received probation each time. When I asked him if he had ever had a "legal" job David replied: "in my neighborhood, people don't have jobs." When I asked what kind of people lived in his neighborhood, David replied: "dealers, prostitutes, users, killers, robbers, home-invaders."

At sixteen years old, David said he and some friends broke into the home of a known drug dealer and robbed him of "$50,000 in cash and two kilos of dope." During the home invasion, David used the gun his grandfather had given him and shot the homeowner in the leg. He was never caught for the incident. David said he kept robbing people because it became an addiction. He claimed that he enjoyed having total control over people, especially women, but he never did it for sexual pleasure.

David was arrested for the current charge when he stole a car from a used car lot. He was driving the car with some friends and was pulled over by the police. He said when the police asked for his license and registration, he tried to run. David did not get far before the police caught and arrested him. I asked David what he would have to do to avoid coming back to prison and he answered: "lose my 'I don't give a fuck' attitude." David also said he would like to go to a halfway house where there would be some freedom but also a system of accountability before going back to his neighborhood. However, he indicated that the halfway houses in his area are filled with just as much crime as on the streets. He said these could be improved by having parole and probation officers come to the offenders, rather than the offenders having to go to them and that offenders should have the choice to go to one of the halfway houses but should not be able to leave once they are there. Finally, he said that in prison, "they should have a wall of achievement so we can see our progress."

Ultimately, however, David was not confident that he would be able to stay out of prison. When I asked him what advice he would give to someone like himself his answer was: "slow down. This is not an experience you want. They don't treat us like we're human."

David's admission that "they," prison staff, don't treat the inmates like they're human is reflected in the 'Pathway to Change' program's insistence that the inmates use performance theater to act out their mistakes in front of other inmates and staff members. Though this part of the program is only one aspect of life in prison that many of us would consider troubling if we were forced to engage it, the emphasis in the program on public degradation is acute. It is unlikely that most grown adults would willingly consent to playing out skits with colleagues to learn a lesson about their personalities. These lessons are not the "team building" exercises employers sometimes use to build rapport and trust within a workplace. Further, the inmates are not on a company retreat; they are locked behind bars and their participation is entirely involuntary. So, whatever many of us would consider degrading in everyday life is heightened, highlighted and painfully exposed in the prison environment. The lack of respect for the intensity of the prison environment as well as for the inherent absence of power the inmates have over their own selves is most evident here. The gross displays of humiliation forced on the inmates by the program can only contribute to the sense that David does not feel that he is treated like a human.

Reiterating the story about Patty and her problems as a way to encourage the inmates to learn to communicate may, in fact, teach them a lesson about expressing themselves. But, it is also easy to see how repeated, forced instances of such exercises also serve to further divide the inmates from the staff, especially if the inmates feel that they are not afforded basic respect as human beings. The coercive control in these instances of degradation is divisive and most certainly serves to emphasize the huge chasm that separates the inmates/performers from the staff/audience.

The performance aspect here, in particular, exemplifies Goffman's (1963) observations of the "minstrelization" of stigmatized individuals (110). The phenomenon occurs when a stigmatized person exaggerates his shortcomings, playing into his audience's expectations about how he should act based on how they expect his stigma to influence his everyday performances. Stigmatized individuals often engage in this process to buffer anticipated reactions from their audience, thus allowing them a greater measure of control in the management of the information they convey about themselves. In the case of the inmates required to perform in this program, minstrelization is coerced and forced so that the performances the inmates give are reactive, rather than proactive, thus negating any possibility that they could use their performance for self-protection.

The need to feel respected as thinking, feeling human beings was a common theme in the inmates' narratives. Perhaps the lack of respect the inmates felt outside of prison made the need for it inside that much more acute. For James, giving and receiving respect is not simply a matter of general decency, but it is also a potential key to his success on the outside. James is a twenty-four-year-old Black man from a large city in the Midwest. James dropped out of high school in the eleventh grade but plans on continuing his education to receive his GED. James grew up with fourteen brothers and sisters and first experienced drugs by watching his older brothers smoke marijuana. James said his brothers told him not to do drugs so he hid his drug use and began smoking marijuana at nine years old. James is in prison on a seven-year sentence for felony possession of drugs and has served twenty-one months to date.

When I asked James to tell me about his life growing up he said: "with a family so big like that there's no consequences. We didn't live in no ghetto – we lived around all white people. I had high taste and I didn't get it from home." He said the most important people in his life as a child were his mom and dad because "everything they ever told me came true." Now, the most important people in his life are his mom and his sons. James' father died five years ago. James was reluctant to speak of his father but when I asked him who or what he believed was the main reason why he is currently incarcerated, James answered: "the person who told me to play football for four years and I never once saw him in the stands." I asked James if he thought he would ever have to come back to prison and he said: "I don't want this to be the fate of my life. I'm gonna try my hardest but if things don't go my way, you never know. This place made me sick. I've missed so many things."

Because James is serving time for possessing enough drugs to warrant a felony charge, I asked him if he believed he had a drug problem, James replied: "I don't have a drug problem, I have a money problem. I'm high on life. Only thing I can see coming back here for is money – selling drugs." I asked him if his girlfriend is supportive of him and if she could help keep him from coming back and James replied: "I do love her enough to not come back but who's to say what happens when I get out of here?"

Finally, I asked James what he thought could help keep him and others like him from ending up back in prison for a second time. James said that people need "help to get jobs," but mostly it would help if:

> you'd get to talk to someone who doesn't judge. You build up a lot of stuff in here, it'd be nice to get it out. You don't feel like you can talk to nobody in here. This stuff I just told you I wouldn't have told to anyone. This conversation we're having right here will stick with me because you didn't judge.

James' indication that our conversation will "stick" with him because I did not judge him is also an indication that some of the other information he receives in prison will not stay with him on the outside because it is delivered without respect. James clearly and articulately expressed a primary key to his potential success on the outside in his wish to be heard and respected. Prison programs like this neglect from the outset the basic human need for individuals to feel like they are understood. According to David and James, prison staff members do not treat the inmates with respect. That principle extends to the content of the 'Pathway to Change' program through the involuntary, mandatory and public performances highlighting the inmates' mistakes and inadequacies. The performances mandated in the program never require the inmates to construct a skit about the positive choices they've made or the good decisions they managed in the face of mountainous opposition; rather, they highlight the moments in life where the inmates failed and use those failures as the basis for the construction of these public shaming rituals.

Regardless of the lesson the inmates are supposed to learn, there is a blatant disregard in the program for privacy and respect through the methods it uses to deliver its messages. Teaching students in a class a lesson by encouraging levity through games or performances is not, in itself, a poor pedagogical technique. Using those methods to teach prison inmates about their personalities, however, neglects one of the most basic elements of prison life in the impossibility of the inmates' right to refuse. If they don't perform the skit or play the game, they don't complete the lesson. If they don't complete the lesson, they fail the course. If they fail the course, they don't get out of prison. More than that, however, the discipline enforced by the prison is not simply one where the consequences are so clear-cut. The inmates know they must pass the course in order to be released and so most of them do graduate from the program. The question now is not whether forced participation is another way to enact discursive discipline, but how the multiple layers of that disciplinary tactic manage to subtly cut away at the real men who live and have lived through the events that made them who they are today.

The program, the institution, the Department of Corrections, the state and the taxpayers in the alignment of their wants and the provision of their services neglect to consider the consequences of enacting discursive discipline on human subjects. The discursive project here involves highlighting the distinction between "good" non-criminals and "bad" prison inmates under the guise of processes that resemble unification. The state uses humiliation and degradation to put the inmates 'in their place.' In doing so, it draws a heavy line between *them* (bad men who made bad choices) and everyone else. The use of degradation and lack of respect for human dignity is used as a tactic to drive them further away from the general population. The contradiction, however, is that in further distinguishing the inmates from the "good" citizens, the state simultaneously aligns its goals with those of the taxpayers by claiming that it is actually making the inmates *more* like productive citizens (Bosworth, 2007). The state justifies its use of punitive practices by packaging them as rehabilitative programs designed to "produce employable offenders." This statement satisfies the people who vote for political leaders and give their tax dollars to state-funded recidivism reduction initiatives enough that the contradictory nature of the programs in use are largely irrelevant, so long as the meta-narratives produced by the state manage to align with those that distinguish American values. Essentially, it doesn't matter *how* we break prison inmates of their bad thinking patterns so long as they are broken down enough to become fully aware of their lowered social statuses and their differentiation from everyone else. Degradation is a method by which punitive discipline is delivered and there is nothing the inmates can do but go along with the show, even at the risk of losing who they are entirely.

Disconnection

Perhaps one of the most confounding problems with the 'Pathway to Change' program is in the vast inconsistencies inherent to the internal structure of the lessons. The issue of disconnection between the stated objectives of the lessons and the methods used in the exercises is evident in most of the lessons. Maintaining internal consistency within the lessons becomes problematic, as the language of the manual seems to initially address one thing, but fails to adequately follow through with the original objective or concept by the conclusion of the exercise. The result of this disconnection between the stated objectives and the methods used to achieve them calls into question the validity, reliability and integrity of the individual lessons themselves. At times, it seems that the author of the program manual intended the lesson to teach a particular concept, but was unable to connect the concept to an appropriate exercise.

Recall in Lesson 2, the manual instructs the teacher to provide the inmates with a 'personality styles test' and arrange them into similar personality groups. One of the activities that follows the test indicates that the inmates should create and perform a skit they feel would convince a member of an opposite personality group to consider the effects drug abuse has had on their lives. Here, Lesson 2 makes a leap that is quite difficult to follow. By beginning with personality tests and value assessments and ending with a skit about drug use, the lesson's messages are highly disconnected. There is no explanation; no connection made to link personality types to the behavior of drug use. Cognitive-behavioral therapy often begins by asking the participant to step back and examine their thoughts to reveal unhealthy or flawed patterns and attitudes. Then, therapists typically link those thoughts to very specific problem behaviors in which the individual has engaged, such as compulsive cleaning or shoplifting (Beck et al., 2004). However, the 'Pathway to Change' program in no way links the thinking patterns of drug users to the behavior of actually taking drugs. In fact, the issue of drug use seems like merely an afterthought, thrown into the lesson to lend it some element of supposed relevance to prison inmates. The issue, of course, is that drug addiction is an incredibly real problem with which most of the inmates in this study continue to struggle.

For instance, take John, a thirty-four-year-old White male. He is a high-school graduate and divorced. John is from a rural area in the Midwest and he has four children aged seven to sixteen with two different women. John is currently in prison for the possession of methamphetamine.

John said the first time he tried drugs he was seventeen years old and he has done crank (methamphetamine) ever since. John's current incarceration is the result of an arrest eight months ago. John claimed that he was partying with a friend and her husband at their house. They were doing meth and marijuana when the husband and wife began fighting. To avoid getting caught in the middle, John left the house to take a walk. It was dark out and John was high on meth. He said he was walking down the street, texting on his cell phone when a police officer passed him. Immediately, John thought the officer had been dispatched to his friends' house because they were fighting. Seconds later, however, John heard a voice over a loudspeaker say "pedestrian safety check." When the officer asked John what he was doing out so late, John told the officer it was none of his business. At that, the officer exited his vehicle and John began to run. He ran eight or ten blocks when the officer caught up with him and shot two tazers into John. John hit the ground and was handcuffed by the police. He was charged with possession of methamphetamine, possession of drug paraphernalia, fleeing and eluding and failure to appear in court for a previous warrant on which John owed $7,000 in child support. I asked John to tell me about his history of drug use and he said: "the thought of addiction never even came to my mind" and "I've seen it [drug use] turn some good people into monsters." John said he enjoyed doing crank because "you could stay up for a week and not even know it."

Most of his life John maintained a job packaging medical equipment at a warehouse and said he was able to go to work every day because of the meth. John said he "was a disciplined addict." After John got married to his youngest child's mother he was able to quit using drugs for a couple of months at a time but he always went back to doing meth after staying clean. According to John: "my problem is saying no in the beginning." He says he "couldn't resist it, but can stop any time."

When I asked him what he will do about drug addiction when he is released from prison, John replied: "the thing that scares me the most is seeing someone I know with drugs." For John, resisting the initial allure of starting to do drugs again is the most difficult part of staying clean and also of staying out of prison. I asked John if he thought he would ever have to come back to prison and he said he didn't know if he would ever see the inside of a prison again but he was sure he would not come back for committing a new crime. John said he believed most people end up back in prison because they test positive for drugs while they are on probation or parole. He believes that if he is sent back to prison it will be for that reason.

Finally, I asked John to tell me who or what he thought was the main reason why he ended up having to serve time in prison. John replied: "I got myself here – it's up to me to stay out; I don't blame the judge or the cops." I asked him what he would do to stay out of prison in the future and he said: "stay away from all the bullshit. I just hope one day soon, I can learn the word 'no.'"

John's hope that someday he can learn the word "no" indicates that he may be willing and open to doing so. The 'Pathway to Change' manual, however, neglects to link how an individual's personality is in any way connected to the social and behavioral factors of drug use and the physiological elements of addiction. Simply telling someone like John about his personality type seems wholly inadequate in helping him learn to say "no" to drugs. Compared with the experiences John has gone through in his life, putting on a performance skit about his personality with a group of other prison inmates falls woefully short of addressing his needs as an admitted methamphetamine addict once he is released. The inmates' need to make connections between their thoughts and behaviors is well illustrated in Jay's story.

Jay is a twenty-six-year-old Latino man who grew up in a large city in South America. He came to the United States to live with his mother when he was seventeen years old. Jay has served ten months on the current charge and is currently in prison for the conviction of his fifth DWI (driving while intoxicated).

At eighteen, he got his first DWI and paid the necessary fines. He found a job working in a food factory and two years later received his second DWI. He was sentenced to five weekends in jail and three years of probation. A week later, Jay got his third DWI and received another two years of probation and five more weekends in jail. Jay stayed out of trouble for four years but at twenty-four received his fourth DWI and was sentenced to two years in prison. He did five months, was released, worked for eight months and got his fifth DWI. He has currently served ten months in prison and will be released in approximately three months.

I asked Jay who or what was the reason why he is currently in prison and he answered: "stupidity. This isn't me. I don't like to be locked up." I asked Jay what he would have to do to stay out of prison and he said: "stay busy, work, think of my little girl, go to court, go to church." Finally, I asked Jay if he believes he is an alcoholic. Jay replied: "no, I don't think so."

The thought that a man with five convictions for driving while intoxicated does not believe that he has an alcohol addiction is likely baffling for most of us. Perhaps one of the most clear-cut cases for cognitive restructuring, Jay's thoughts and actions obviously are at odds. Yet, the 'Pathway to Change' manual would have him simply act out a skit to encourage other inmates to think about the effects of drugs on their lives in a one-hour classroom exercise. Although Jay is required to complete drug and alcohol abuse classes while in prison and also when he is released, the 'Pathway to Change' class is a missed opportunity to realistically employ cognitive therapy in relation to the disease of alcoholism.

The disconnection between the goals of the lessons and the expected outcomes is evident. Many of the stated objectives have little to do with the methods used in the class to obtain them. The inmates are given information, forced to complete an in-class exercise and expected to individually make the link between the stated purpose of the lesson and the activity itself. With no guidance to speak of and little connection between the objectives and the outcomes in the lessons, the 'Pathway to Change' class becomes entirely pointless. It seems quite a stretch indeed to claim that anything about this class resembles therapy. The methods are shoddy, the linkages incomplete and the lessons wholly confusing. When the reality of the situation is that some of the men forced to take this class are truly suffering from delusions regarding the actual state of their psychological and physical addictions to drugs and alcohol, not only does this class not address those issues, but it further muddies the waters in its inconsistency, disconnection and lack of follow-through.

Unfortunately, the issue of disconnectedness of the lessons' objectives and the content of the material did not end in Lesson 2. In Lesson 16, "Your Hot Buttons," (35–7) the class is told to create a list of things other people often do that drives them "crazy." From the lists, the inmates are to pick the funniest activity and create a play to perform for the rest of the class. An interesting exercise in self-reflection, Lesson 16 seems to be on to something. The problem, though, is that the stated objective of the lesson is "to help participants understand why violent behaviors often show up in intimate relationships and how to avoid this destructive pattern of behavior." Violent and destructive behaviors, however, are not discussed in the lesson. The activity is posed and the inmates complete it, but there is no connection to violent behavior or intimate relationships anywhere in the lesson. The activity ends by posing a series of questions asking the inmates what they can do when someone pushes their 'hot buttons,' but it never actually explains how those questions link back to the content of the class activity.

Again, as with drug and alcohol problems, we can see that the trouble here has to do with the fact that violence, abuse, threats and anger are real issues that many of the men address in their stories. For instance, Jesse is twenty-one years old, White and from the suburban area of a large midwestern city. Jesse said he was the leader of a gang of friends who were all expelled for bringing drugs to school and fighting, and he said he has been in a drug-filled environment since the day he was born. He has always witnessed his father doing marijuana and tried it himself for the first time at ten years old. Jesse said that when he was young, he wanted to grow up to be a sniper.

Jesse claimed that he was kicked out of his parents' house when he was a teenager because he told his father he did not want to play football anymore. His father hit him and Jesse stabbed his dad with a knife. His mother packed his bags and Jesse went to live with his girlfriend's mother and her partner. Jesse said he began doing meth at this time and when his girlfriend became pregnant he started work at a fast food restaurant.

As a young man, Jesse received probation for various charges including drug possession, fighting, driving under the influence and driving with a suspended license. While on probation, Jesse assaulted a man at a party. He was drinking excessive amounts of alcohol and doing a combination of drugs when he felt threatened by the man. Jesse said he beat the man until the police arrived. Jesse was arrested and sentenced to three years in prison. When I asked Jesse why he believes he is in prison he said: "because I like to fight."

Jesse said that in order to help keep people from coming back to prison, the state needs to help set them up with a job and a home when they are released. Jesse's release date has been continually set back because he lacks a suitable "home plan," or place to stay for the six months following his release. I asked Jesse what keeps him going day to day and he replied: "if I didn't have my son, I'd probably be dead by now."

Quite clearly, Jesse is a young man with some serious issues related to violent behavior, controlling his temper and dealing with abuse as a child. Lesson 16 provides the several alternatives to violence the inmates should use, including taking a time-out, refraining from the use of drugs or alcohol, getting something to eat or going by themselves for a walk or jog (36).

After reading Jesse's story about stabbing his own abusive father with a knife and beating a man at a party until the police pulled him off, the advice in the 'Pathway to Change' program would seem almost comical if it weren't so disturbing. Obviously, though, it's not a joke and the state of Missouri spends its time, money and resources on maintaining this program. The disconnection in this program is not simply internal to the lessons themselves, but between the class and reality as well. It is as if the manual's author has no experience with the realities of crime and addiction or poverty and desperation, yet fancies himself an expert on the lives of prison inmates. In any case, the Missouri Department of Corrections is certainly convinced of the credibility of this program.

Lesson 19 in the 'Pathway to Change' manual takes up the unique issue of "Understanding Sexuality" (41–3). The stated objective of Lesson 19 is "to help participants understand the difference between sex, love and intimacy." The lesson attempts to help the inmates achieve this objective by instructing the teacher to divide the class into groups and play selections from a variety of "love songs." The groups are then to decide if the song is about sex, love or intimacy. No further explanation linking the method to the objective is provided and no additional information is given.

The disconnection between the content of the manual and the inmates' realities is most evident here. Take Andrew, a twenty-three-year-old White man from a large urban area in the North. He received his high school diploma from an alternative school where he was placed at thirteen years of age after molesting an eight-year-old girl. Andrew wants to pursue a bachelor's degree in business management.

Andrew's troubles began when he was thirteen years old and he was caught molesting a girl in his neighborhood. He was sent to a detention home and completed school there. He was released to his mother's custody when he was sixteen years old but said he was really on his own. At twenty-one years old, Andrew was homeless and out of money. He began stealing electronics from businesses and homes to pawn and eventually he stole a car. He and a friend went "joy riding" in the stolen car and wrecked it. The police were called and both friends "snitched" on each other. Andrew received a three-year prison sentence and served five months. Upon his release, Andrew was required to meet certain conditions of parole. As a result of his sex offense, Andrew claims that he was not allowed to be on the Internet, have a romantic relationship, leave the state or be around children. Andrew said he broke all of these conditions when he used the Internet to meet his current wife who had children of her own. Andrew did not go to meetings with his parole officer and routinely babysat his future wife's children. He was arrested for violating his parole one year ago. During his current incarceration, Andrew and his wife got married in the prison chapel. His wife works as an exotic dancer and currently supports Andrew and her own children.

Andrew admitted that he still has a difficult time around children because he continues to have thoughts and desires that he is afraid will lead to another molestation. He said that therapy and prison classes have helped and he prides himself on the fact that: "I can now watch Huggies [diaper] commercials and not get excited by the kids on TV." I asked Andrew who or what he believes to be the main reason he is in prison and he answered: "I take half responsibility." Finally, I asked him what he would do to stay out of prison and Andrew replied: "follow all the bureaucratic bullcrap." At the time of this writing, Andrew was expected to be getting out of prison in two months.

Andrew was the only individual in my sample who admitted to committing a sex offense. It is a stretch to believe, however, that Lesson 19 in the mandatory 'Pathway to Change' class Andrew took helped him discern between sex, love and intimacy. With no connection to the reality of the struggles some of these men face, the program falters.

Lesson 10 (21–2) encourages the inmates to understand how becoming more successful is related to creating a positive self-image. It attempts to accomplish this goal by instructing the teacher to have the inmates pick some items of clothing from a bag, put them on, and explain to the class how those items reflect the image they want others to see. Lesson 10 also suggests having the inmates cut pictures from magazines and use paste to create a collage of the attributes they most want to convey. The lesson attempts to connect a positive self-image by drawing the inmates' attention to the aspects of themselves they most want others to see. The connection, though, is lost when the program neglects to explain how to bring these positive characteristics to the fore in reality. It certainly does not explain what the inmates are to do in the real world when they don't have scissors and paste or a bag full of clothing with which to express themselves. Indeed, the program also does not explain exactly how a positive self-image plays a role in reducing the likelihood that they will recidivate. This problem is best articulated in Tim's story.

Tim is a twenty-one-year-old White man from a small town. He dropped out of high school in the eleventh grade but received his GED in prison. When he was eight years old he witnessed his father smoking marijuana and tried it for the first time when he was fifteen. Tim has also used cocaine, alcohol and ecstasy. He has currently served one year on a four-year sentence for burglary.

Tim's history with the law began when he was sixteen years old. He began getting high on marijuana and alcohol on a regular basis and started breaking into cars, stealing money and stereos and pawning them for money to buy drugs. He said that he tried to get a job and said he "put in a bunch of applications" but no one would hire him. Eventually, Tim began breaking into cars and homes again to make money. Soon after, Tim's friend suggested that they break into college dorm rooms to steal electronics and money. They broke into half a dozen dorm rooms in the middle of the night and were caught by the police. Tim said of the incident: "I just kept thinking, eventually I'll quit. I didn't even really want to do it." Tim received a four-year sentence in prison, has served one year and is scheduled for release in four months.

I asked Tim what was the primary reason why he is in prison and he said: "probably me. I'll buy drugs and alcohol before I'd buy food." I asked how prison has changed him and Tim replied: "I've been trying to teach myself to speak up. I used to look at everything in a negative way, now I'd like to think I'm a positive person." Finally, I wanted to know what would help keep Tim from coming back to prison. He answered: "I've got a lot more family support now than I did before. If I come back it will be on a parole violation."

For Tim, having a positive attitude seems to help improve his outlook on life. He prides himself on no longer looking at his life negatively, but teaching himself to speak up and become more positive. But, Tim also seems to struggle in making the connection between improving his attitude and staying out of prison. He is unsure whether or not he will return but believes that if he does it will be because of a parole violation, rather than for something that he could (presumably) control by changing his attitude. Tim's inability to connect a positive attitude and self-image to the rigors of parole is certainly not addressed in the 'Pathway to Change' program. In fact, this disconnection is exacerbated in the program, rather than realistically addressed and resolved.

The disconnectedness of the program's goals and its methods is spread across the lessons. It is no wonder the inmates often express confusion and frustration in their stories when referencing the issues the manual dredges up, but neglects to effectively conclude; recall John's statement: "I just hope one day soon I can learn the word 'no.'" The truth is, the inmates don't know how to help themselves; if they did, it is unlikely they would have ended up in prison to begin with. It's evident that within their stories they seek guidance and concrete solutions to some of the bitter realities facing them on the outside. Perhaps one of the greatest failures of the 'Pathway to Change' program is in its unfulfilled promises. By failing to connect the issues the inmates face with realistic means and plans for overcoming them, the program simply teases the inmates into believing that they are actually learning something useful.

For Henry and Milovanovic's (1996) constitutive criminology, a similar issue takes shape in the way the whole of the criminal justice system constructs realities divergent from the localized and temporal social conditions of the actors it addresses:

> In order to sustain abstractly constructed distinctions, discursive constructions are made applicable to events, in spite of the contradictory evidence that comes from renewed micro-interaction. Contradictory evidence and potential disruptions are engendered by the internal transfer of messages, a basis of instability that is best negotiated by framing it into already understood narrative constructs that 'beg' us to make old reaffirming sense of new nonsense (69).

The Department of Corrections' use of standardized cognitive self-change programs in prison as a way to perpetuate its overarching goal of further separating the "good" taxpaying public from the "bad" prison inmate Other supports Henry and Milovanovic's observation of its contradictory and unstable discursive frames. Particularly, the 'Pathway to Change' program provides us with a ripe empirical example of this phenomenon. The 'discursive constructions' apparent throughout the program engender self-blame and degradation and are made applicable to the inmates' lives despite contradictory evidence of any real connection to the social processes and interactions they actually experience. The more the inmates are made to repeat the mantras of the pre-formed narratives given to them through institutional means, the more they seem to make sense. The narratives are bound within familiar and predictable frames; the inmates, just like anyone else, understand that there should be a separation between good and evil, that taking responsibility for one's failures is a way to engage patriotism and those who break the law deserve punishment. These narrative boundaries limit discursive and cognitive space in such a way that to deny them further pushes the inmates outside the realm of conformity; and, above all else, prison is a place where conforming means freedom. In everyday life, this notion of refusing to engage the pre-set boundaries of social scripts and narratives may, at a minimum, mean that the non-conformist would be met with some manner of informal social control or shaming. In the prison, where these scripts and narratives are not just suggestions for social conduct but required anthems of solidarity to the established social order, the consequence is the continued refusal of physical, mental and social freedoms. This type of denial of freedom for refusing to engage the master narrative in prison is discursive discipline.

Self-blame, degradation and disconnection illustrate three problematic themes primarily found in the ways the lessons themselves are structured. The internal issues relevant to realistically accessing stated objectives, the methods used for employing exercises and the rhetoric and internal discourses pertinent to the way the inmates are expected to refer to their own stories represent a gap between the program initiatives and the inmates' narratives. In the next chapter, this gap widens with the inclusion of a general detachment from reality and expertly created knowledge more characteristic of the broad divide evident between state-mediated meta-narrative and the inmates' lived realities.

Note

1 Wayne's story was first printed in Schlosser, J. (2008). Issues in interviewing inmates: Navigating the methodological landmines of prison research. *Qualitative Inquiry, 14*(8), 1500–525. DOI:10.1177/1077800408318325. Thanks to Sage for their kind permission to reproduce this material in this chapter.

References

Beck, A. T., Freeman, A. & Davis, D. (2004). *Cognitive therapy of personality disorders.* New York: The Guilford Press.

Bosworth, M. (2007). Creating responsible prisoners: Federal admission and orientation packs. *Punishment and Society, 9*(67), 67–85.

Fox, K. (1999). Changing violent minds: Discursive correction and resistance in the cognitive treatment of violent offenders in prison. *Social Problems, 46*(1), 88–103.

Garfinkel, H. (1956). Conditions of successful degradation ceremonies. *American Journal of Sociology, 61*(5), 420–4.

Goffman, E. (1963). *Stigma: Notes on the management of spoiled identity.* New York: Simon and Schuster.

Henry, S. & Milovanovic, D. (1996). *Constitutive criminology: Beyond postmodernism.* Thousand Oaks, CA: Sage Publications.

'Pathway to Change'. (2005). *Introductory manual.* Clime International.

Schlosser, J. (2008). Issues in interviewing inmates: Navigating the methodological landmines of prison research. *Qualitative Inquiry, 14*(8), 1500–525. DOI:10.1177/1077800408318325

7 The divide

"[I] used crack as another form of currency."

Chad, 24

Beyond content: structural problems in program design

The next two issues, detachment from reality and the imposition of expert knowledge, illustrate more broad-based issues with the 'Pathway to Change' program in general. These problems span across the program but occur most prominently in several specific lessons. Here, the gap between the program content and the inmates' narratives widens and creates a deeper divide that more broadly characterizes the meta-narrative of the state in general. The disconnection between the proponents of expert knowledge and the lived realities of the inmates is most evident along these two themes.

Beyond the program, however, we'll also see in this chapter that the two issues found in the empirical example also embody an affirmative postmodernist conception of the legal structure in general. This position leads with the idea that the power relations evident in our legal and criminal justice systems are not separate from those governing society at large, nor do they merely influence one another passively. The relationships of power and the decisions made in both state law and social law are mutually interrelated; one affects the other to the point that neither can be considered autonomously (Henry & Milovanovic, 1996). Expert knowledge and the enmeshing of individual realities with contradictory common meta-narratives did not originate in the criminal justice and legal systems, nor do they operate separately from them. These processes of social control circulate in and out of many governing institutions and moral landscapes relevant to our modern world (Reiman, 2009). The affirmative postmodern position is most applicable here when we see that the socio-legal processes that carve and distinguish our criminal justice institutions are the same ones that define the whole of our social lives. Extending that critique, it is necessary then to question who among us is really free if the processes we use to govern and discipline our convicted criminals are the very ones by which we govern and discipline ourselves.

There is, in fact, no distinction between how these processes are enacted upon our inmates and how we use them in our daily lives through any of our educational, political, religious or social institutions (Foucault, 1979). Two of these processes, the imposition of expert knowledge and the detachment of meta-narratives from individual realities in particular, will be analyzed here in direct relation to their empirical expression in prison. It is important to understand, however, that the affirmative postmodern position indicating that the processes of power and control present in the legal system are also wholly evident as overarching power strategies in our other social systems is what will allow us to see these two processes operating simultaneously and in cooperation beyond their situated expression here.

Detached from reality

Detachment from reality is a general characteristic of many in-prison programs and, indeed, an issue most of the inmates mentioned in their narratives. Detachment from reality represents a larger problem than the disconnection between the stated objectives of a particular lesson with the methods used to attempt to achieve those objectives. Here, the problem becomes a detachment in the lesson's main themes and exercises from the reality of life for the inmates both inside and outside of prison. The lessons use weak examples and unrealistic scenarios in an attempt to relate the cognitive self-change rhetoric to "real life." In fact, the examples of real scenarios used in the lessons often seem like they were not written for prison inmates at all because they are so divorced from anything the inmates state they've experienced. Often, the examples are mundane, watered down versions of "actual" cases that almost seem too sophomoric to be taken seriously by anyone, let alone prison inmates.

This theme of detachment from reality begins in Lesson 4 ("It's All in the Attitude"). Here, the teacher should "help participants understand the relationship between their values, attitude and actions and how they are affected by their personality" (9–10). To complete this task, the class should evaluate the descriptions of five fictional people and determine who has the best values and who has the worst values. First, "Lynne the Late" is hurrying to get to work on time and strikes a child with her car. She then speeds away from the scene without checking on the victim. "Chris the Carefree" believes he may have been exposed to AIDS but refuses to get tested. He continues having unprotected sex with multiple partners without telling them about his past exposure. "Pat the President" sells spoiled meat to poor people. He overcharges them for the meat and becomes rich off the profits. "Gari the Gossip" spreads rumors about other people for her own gain. Finally, "Willie the Witness" saw a crime happen but fears for his own safety so does not contact the police. As a result, an innocent person is charged with the crime.

After reading these stories, the inmates are instructed to rank each character in order of best values to worst values. The manual warns the instructor that there is no correct ordering of the characters and to be careful not to devalue any inmate's answer.

The examples provided in Lesson 4 effectively illustrate the institutional detachment from the real, experienced lives of the inmates. The prison, the program and, particularly, this lesson strip all experiences of context. By providing the inmates with two or three simple sentences to describe entirely complicated situations, the manual cuts away any ambiguity, subjectivity, environmental influence or contextual liability. It leaves behind a skeletal representation of "reality" and forces the inmates to choose which of them is worse. The effect of stripping out context mirrors the experiences of inmates themselves during their participation in the program. They are repeatedly asked to ignore the extenuating or contributing circumstances that may have influenced their own life experiences. The result of this detachment from reality introduces a version of decision making that is entirely unrealistic. People rarely make random decisions entirely alone, with no outside influence. Yet, in each of the five scenarios the manual provides, the characters (and, thus, the inmates) exist in a social vacuum, minimally influenced by anything other than their own "bad" choices. The construction of scenarios involving polarized and extreme examples encourages the establishment of thinking patterns far removed from those that are likely or even possible in real-world situations.

Take Ronald, a thirty-one-year-old Black man from a "rough urban area" of a large city. Ronald said of his hometown: "there were killings, prostitutes, drugs, carjackings, abuse – I come from one of the hardest cities in the world." He lived there with his mother and ten siblings. His mother shot and killed Ronald's father in self-defense when Ronald was ten years old. Both Ronald's parents are now dead and when I asked him how he felt about his childhood, Ronald replied: "that's the hand I was dealt. I'm thirty-one years old and I can recall some things in my head that still make me teary." According to Ronald, his mother was a registered nurse and a thief: "she was a really good booster." He said his father was a beautician, a hustler and a pimp. The most important person in his life as a child was his mother because "we had been through a lot." The most important person to Ronald now is his wife because: "we understand each other. We understand the concept of love." Ronald has three children and has been to prison five times.

The first time Ronald went to prison was for violating his probation on a previous charge. Ronald served ten months in prison and was released on parole. According to Ronald, after he was out of prison for a few months, "the cops planted some dope on me" and he received five more years in prison. Ronald served three years and was released again. In 2004 he was caught with half a kilogram of crack cocaine. I asked Ronald where he was when he got caught and he replied: "at the Taco Bell." I commented that Taco Bell seemed an unlikely place to get caught with drugs and he replied: "yea, I shoulda made a run for the border!"

I asked him what he will do to keep from going back to prison for a sixth time and he replied: "I'm gonna try to do everything different. She [his wife] can't keep me out, only I can keep myself out. When I mess up, I mess up to the fullest." Finally, I asked Ronald what the biggest obstacle for him will be when he is released. Ronald replied: "knowing what the right thing is to do but not doing it."

The strong tendency in the 'Pathway to Change' program on creating unrealistic scenarios devoid of context or adequate framing stands in stark contrast to the issues Ronald faced. The trials of "Lynne the Late," "Chris the Carefree," "Pat the President," "Gari the Gossip" and "Willie the Witness," as representative of real life problems, seem more like a joke than a teaching tool in the face of Ronald's admission that his mother was a thief, a booster and, ultimately, the murderer of his pimp father. The "decisions" made by the fictional characters portrayed in the manual are light years removed from the lives of these men. This feature of creating "representative" scenarios in a social and contextual vacuum is typical of "therapeutic" authority in prison. The authors of these programs, as well as the administrators of prisons, are far enough removed from the inmates' realities that it is unlikely they could fabricate teaching moments even closely related to life on the streets. The result is an insulting, unrealistic representation of make-believe reality that could potentially have the effect of causing more harm than good. If inmates in prison cannot relate to the examples provided in quasi-therapeutic programs like this, they are at risk of shutting down entirely and losing anything of value they might have taken from the class.

Unrealistic examples of "problems" the inmates may face come to the fore again (Lesson 12, "Decisions," 25–6). The goal of the lesson is "to help participants understand their personal preferences in the decision making process." The lesson begins by asking the instructor to break the class into groups. Each group is instructed to come up with solutions to a variety of problems. In "Problem A," some people are using the same space regularly and have left it a mess for the past week. They are told they must clean the space or they may lose the right to continue to use it. "Problem B" indicates that neighborhood drinking water is contaminated with gasoline. The owner of a nearby gas station claims he replaced the pumps recently, so the contamination cannot be his fault. In "Problem C," a married couple can't agree on what type of new car they should buy. A sick hospital patient in "Problem D" has undergone many tests, but the doctors are still unsure of his condition. He can be given a new drug that may save his life, but if the doctors are wrong, the drug will kill the patient. They must try the drug within the next 30 minutes, or the patient will likely die anyway. In "Problem E," three astronauts in a space shuttle are at risk because one of them is eating and drinking more than his fair share of the rations. Finally, in "Problem F" the inmates are told that they are the director of a state prison and a new group of inmates has arrived. However, there are not enough beds and they can't be sent elsewhere.

Astronauts in a space capsule, contaminated drinking water and the burdens of a prison warden in no way relate to the realities of poverty and crime in the neighborhoods many of these inmates lived. *Their* stories are constructed of very different identity moments; the problems they faced on the outside are much more personal and specific than the "problems" outlined in Lesson 12.

Take Joseph, a forty-two-year-old White man who has been in and out of trouble his entire life. This is his first time serving a prison sentence but he has been on probation multiple times and on the run from various warrants for years. Joseph is divorced and says the most important person in his life now is his mother because she: "lifts my spirits and gives me guidance." Joseph is serving a five-year sentence for violating his probation and for forgery. He has served one year and is scheduled for release in a few weeks.

After having trouble in school, Joseph dropped out and went to live with his father. Joseph did not speak to his mother for twelve years and says he understands now that "single women with children in the 70s had no opportunities." As a teenager, he found himself in much trouble with the law and was placed on probation. After he missed appointments with his probation officer, he hitchhiked to Florida, where he stole a car. Joseph managed to evade arrest but said: "I had no family so I didn't care if I went to prison."

After divorcing his wife, Joseph went to visit his father and moved in with him. One day he found his father's checkbook in his truck and he says: "something just came over me – I'm gonna get that old bastard. He never did nothing for me." So Joseph stole his father's checkbook and took $1,200 from his bank. He was eventually arrested after his ex-wife's grown children alerted the authorities to Joseph's whereabouts and charged him with domestic violence. He is currently serving time in prison for forgery.

When I asked Joseph what he thought might help keep others like himself from coming to prison he said: "you need people who've been in and out of prison to counsel them." Joseph felt that "the younger kids in here respect the older ones" but, he said, "you'll have to have success stories."

As previously mentioned, Joseph has been in and out of trouble for most of his life. His reality includes problems like poverty, abuse and domestic violence. Upon reading about Joseph's struggles with the most important people in his life, it seems illogical to compare his problems with the examples in Lesson 12. A husband and wife unable to decide which car to purchase is a far cry from being reported by your spouse's grown children for abuse. It seems like Joseph has much more serious problems to deal with than figuring out who would be responsible for cleaning up a messy shared space.

We see the issue of detachment from reality again in Lesson 8, "The Source of Real Freedom." The program addresses several important themes, but neglects to adequately relate them to any real-world situation the inmates would likely encounter (17–18). Here, the instructor is prompted to draw a map of an island on the chalkboard. The inmates are then to be told that they are required to re-populate the island and they are to choose where they want to live. The inmates take turns putting their initials on the places in the picture where they want to live. The instructor is then to add geographical markings to the map distinguishing areas such as deserts, mountains, woods and farmland. The inmates are allowed to change where they want to live if they choose. The island map is then to be divided into areas by location and those who "live" in the same areas are broken into groups. Once in their groups, the inmates should answer questions that ask how they would govern their island, how they would punish rule breakers, what freedom means, the difference between rights and privileges and so on. The inmates are asked to compare their fictional island government with the United States. Finally, they are asked to address the key question: "what does a person have to do to be free in this country?" (18–19).

While the program addresses a phenomenon it calls a "mental jail" and asks the inmates to think about the difference between a mental jail and a real jail, it does not provide a real-world link, explanation or analysis of the purpose of the lesson. Inmates are asked to create a fictional government where they decide what rights and privileges citizens there have, but they are not guided to explain their answers or consider the benefits or problems associated with them.

Similarly, Lesson 5, "When I'm Out of Esteem," contributes to a detachment in the lessons from the lived realities of the inmates by creating artificial answers to generic context-free scenarios. Instructors are told to help the inmates examine how having or not having esteem can alter their personalities and the ways they act. The lesson instructs the teacher to play a piece of music with a message that involves self-esteem. The class should then pick out specific verses from the song that made them feel a certain way. The manual suggests using the song *The Greatest Love of All* by Whitney Houston.

Finally, the class is to be broken apart into the "personality groups" from an earlier lesson. Each group is to receive a piece of butcher paper and a pen and answer five questions (11). The instructor is prompted to end class by evaluating how well the inmates are able to discuss how they feel when they act inappropriately. According to the answer key, the correct answer is: "any answer that talks about feeling bad."

In this lesson, a troubling theme running throughout the manual becomes clear: inmates' answers to the lesson's questions are largely irrelevant. The answer key is standardized and general, which allows for the lessons to be distributed to a large group of participants and requires minimal instructor feedback. While certainly a cheap and efficient way of administering armchair psychology to a captive audience, the lack of individualization leads to inattention to personal and specific issues the inmates may need to address. While some measure of generalization is necessary to run any bureaucracy, the fact that their answers simply don't matter is certainly not lost on the inmates. For example, we saw from Andrew, who was convicted of a sex offense, that in order to stay out of prison he simply plans to "follow all the bureaucratic bullcrap." As we'll see, so many of their narratives indicate their overall need to simply be listened to and taken seriously; 'Pathway to Change' provides neither.

This pattern is particularly reflected in Jason's story. Jason is a twenty-four-year-old white man from a rural area in the Midwest. He dropped out of high school in the tenth grade and wants to get his GED. Jason said the first time he did drugs was when he tried marijuana at seven years old with his older sister and some of her friends.

He continued to use marijuana and also tried meth, cocaine, ecstasy, acid, mushrooms and prescription medications. After a short time, Jason began manufacturing his own meth while holding down a job trimming trees. At the age of eighteen, Jason said he began working at a pizza restaurant and delivered pizza and drugs to customers. Jason said he was caught in possession of drugs and stopped taking them because he had to pass urine tests for his probation officer. Jason was clean between the ages of eighteen and twenty-two and said of the time: "I was finally free again."

While on probation, however, Jason was riding in a car with a friend and the police stopped them. Jason's friend had drugs and told the police the drugs were Jason's. Jason went to court and received a four-year prison sentence. When I asked him what would help keep him from coming back to prison, Jason replied: "the thought of being away from my family. I'm kind of glad I went through all this." I asked Jason what, if anything, he would change about his past and he said he "would have never used drugs." Finally, I asked him what people like himself would need to stay out of prison and he said: "they need someone to listen and not judge."

The idea that inmates just want someone to "listen and not judge" stands in stark contrast to the methods used in the program. The fact that the inmates' individual answers to the questions posed in the program don't *really* matter is indicative of the sense of detachment Jason and others seem to feel. Once again, we see the same issues expressed in Bill's story.

Bill is a twenty-one-year-old white man from a suburb of a large city. Bill said his family was middle class and lived in a nice area of town. When he was seven years old, Bill witnessed his father smoke marijuana and when he was fourteen he tried it himself. Bill said he has done marijuana, alcohol, prescription drugs, acid, mushrooms and cocaine. Bill received his current prison sentence when he was high on cocaine and stole an all-terrain vehicle from a barn when he and his friends were camping one night.

Bill said his family has been very supportive. I asked Bill why he thought he was in prison and he said: "if I wasn't high, it wouldn't have happened. The fear could get you caught." I asked him what it was like in prison and he replied: "a lot of these guys in here are idiots. I'm laid back." Bill said what he missed most about home was: "the privacy, walking to the refrigerator, not having to wear shoes." Finally, I asked Bill what might help keep him from ever having to come back to prison. He said: "it seems like the people who are on the right path already have someone to listen to them."

Their stories indicate a longing to be heard. These grown men, convicted criminals, are asking for someone to listen to them. The standard answers provided in the program do not address this need. In fact, our cultural constructions of masculinity in general do not address this need. The desire to talk to another person about personal problems is commonly considered emblematic of weakness, submissiveness and cowardice. These general narrative themes are woven so tightly into the structure of our basic cultural constructions that they are very easy to spot in a place as intensely masculine and violent as a prison. Just like there are right and wrong answers indicated in the program manual, there are also right and wrong answers to the same questions in the more basic social interactions encountered on the outside. If a probation officer, judge or employer took the time to ask these men what would help them become successful citizens, it is highly unlikely that they would answer truthfully. The correct answer for any man, let alone a convicted felon, is most certainly not to ask that someone listen to their problems. So, it is a courageous feat for these inmates to acknowledge that the most successful prisoners, those peers who seem to have the best shot at making it on the outside, are the ones who already have someone who will simply listen and support them. While they aren't "allowed" to directly ask for that type of help for themselves due to the fear of the social repercussions attached to breaking the standardized narrative script, they most certainly acknowledge it as a key component to successful recidivism reduction.

We see this issue of a standardized narrative occurs again in Lesson 6 ("My People," 13–14). Here, the instructor introduces a hypothetical crisis situation to the class and asks them each to make a list of the people they would want to be with them when they had to deal with this crisis. Then, the inmates are required to make another list of people who were with them when they got in trouble and compare the two lists. The manual asks the instructor to "point out that the people who are the best for them are not usually with you when you get in trouble."

This lesson provides a typical cognitive restructuring exercise by juxtaposing what a subject "usually" does with what they know they "should" do. Holding up comparative solutions to addressing a problem can be a fruitful thought experiment. However, the manual makes the problematic assumption that the people the inmates list as individuals they would want to help them through a crisis are not the same people who were also with them when they got in trouble. Nothing indicates what the inmates should do if their two lists are identical or contain most of the same names. In reality, it may very well be the case that the people who negatively influence them are also the people with whom they share the closest bond, trust most and would want by their side in a crisis. In many of the narratives gathered for this project, the inmates indicated that they, in fact, had no legitimately supportive people in their lives. Additionally, many of them also stated that their mothers, fathers, siblings and closest friends were also in prison or were currently involved in criminal activities themselves. The manual does not address any alternative solutions for dealing with such situations. Paul's story provides a striking and articulate contrast to this theme in the program.

Paul is a twenty-six-year-old Black man from the inner city of a large urban area. Paul dropped out of school in the ninth grade but wants to receive his GED someday. While Paul was growing up, his stepfather sold cocaine and marijuana but "he would separate the two when he came home. He was a family man." Paul said the most important person in his life is his grandmother because "there's something she see in me. She tried so hard to get us to see the long-term picture." Paul's mother, stepfather and little brother have all been arrested for drugs.

Paul said the turning point in his life was when his best friend, his cousin, died. Paul said that he and his cousin were inseparable all their lives. They often ran around the neighborhood together and never got into much trouble. When they were fourteen, however, they soon realized that in their neighborhood, "everyone had to be in a gang." The two were not officially affiliated with any gang but one day they were caught wearing the wrong colors in the wrong neighborhood. Paul said gang members started shooting. He and his cousin both started running toward each other and his cousin was shot. Paul said: "he collapsed in my arms and died." Paul showed me the tattoo he got to commemorate his cousin.

After the shooting, Paul was sent to live with an uncle in California but "they were [gang] banging even tougher down there" so six months later he came back to his hometown. Paul moved in with his grandmother and she started to spoil him with money, clothing and jewelry. Paul said he "wasn't learning any responsibility because she never put her foot down." Eventually, however, Paul's grandmother learned that he was selling crack and marijuana and she stopped spoiling him. At eighteen, he chose to move back in with his mother because he didn't want to disrespect his grandmother and because his mom was selling drugs too. He said of his mother: "we were partners." After a few months of living there the police searched the house and they found drugs. Paul received two years supervised probation but said "it was a game, a rush" to keep selling drugs while on probation.

At twenty years old, Paul was off probation and decided that selling drugs was "not a game – got to be serious, be a business man about it." So, Paul made frequent trips to Florida, where he was having ecstasy shipped to him that he would bring back to the Midwest for sale. He said: "I never made money like that before."

After a few years, Paul was caught in possession of drugs again and was sentenced to five years in prison. He has served one year so far and is scheduled for release within a few months as of this writing. I asked Paul how prison had changed him and he said: "prison has made me a believer. The best thing for me to do would be to move to Chicago and start a jewelry store with my uncle." When I asked him who or what was the main reason he was in prison today he replied: "it's all on you as an individual." Finally, I wanted to know what he thought might help other people like himself from coming to prison. Paul said: "experience is the best teacher for some people."

The program sets up family and friends in a dichotomous relationship to the inmate: there are the people the inmates are around when they get in trouble, and there are people who are supportive and helpful. The program constructs both groups as separate and mutually exclusive. Clearly, however, we see from

Paul's story that his own mother was one of his strongest supporters and also his drug-dealing partner. Likewise, his cousin was his best friend but died in Paul's arms because the two were caught in a gang rivalry. As a result, the program sets up an entirely unrealistic representation of the presumed relationship among friends and family to the inmates. This simplistic rendering of interpersonal connections is not a helpful comparison when the intricacies of family relations are so entwined with the complications of a life of crime.

This tension is reflected again in William's story, where we see that his relationships with his mother and now with his stepdaughters help narrate the story of the events in his life and the choices he struggles to make. William is a thirty-year-old high-school dropout. His mother is White, his father is Black and William classifies himself as mixed race. Growing up, William lived with his mother, four sisters, one brother and his mother's various boyfriends in the inner city of a small college town. Convicted and incarcerated for selling drugs, William's brother and a cousin are currently in prison; one of William's sisters also did time for stealing a gun. Currently, William has two cousins, one best friend and an uncle in prison for selling drugs. William has served three years of a seven-year sentence for selling crack to a police informant and is up for release in two months.

William's first experience with drugs occurred when he was eight years old. He witnessed one of his mother's boyfriends doing "wet sticks" (cigarettes laced with PCP, LSD and dipped in embalming fluid). He and his five siblings were in and out of foster care most of their lives. At sixteen, William dropped out of high school because he did not feel like he fit in. Then, at seventeen, William learned from his friends how to drive and stole and wrecked a car he later discovered belonged to a local judge. William served three years in prison for auto theft and became a drug dealer to make money once he was released. William stated that he never believed he would go to prison despite the fact that he knew selling marijuana was illegal. Likewise, William believes that his mother was well aware that he sold drugs but never did anything about it. He was arrested for selling drugs to a police informant and is currently serving his sentence on that charge.

William is still in contact with the people from his old neighborhood and he believes he will continue to sell drugs upon his release, although he wants to stop. His ultimate goal is to get a job and go to Oklahoma to live with his sister and start over. William feels that he is just "too old to keep doing it." William's main concerns at this time are his three stepchildren who are currently eighteen, fifteen and twelve. He worries that his stepdaughters especially will fall into the wrong crowd because the neighborhood where they are living (and where he grew up) is filled with people selling drugs, violence and prostitution. He worries about his daughters being raped and does not allow them to wear make-up. William says he still tries to act as the father figure for his stepchildren despite the fact that he and his wife separated.

When asked what advice William would give someone who was on the path to prison he responded, "coke and ecstasy will eventually ruin a person's life";

however, he believes that "there is nothing wrong with weed." When asked what he would do, if anything, to improve his neighborhood, William said that he felt things might be better if children did not see adults doing drugs. William does not feel that he has had the same opportunities in his life as everyone else because he dropped out of high school and committed a felony at an early age. However, he feels that someday he may try to go to college to study art and sculpting if he can get his life back on track. Asked what he would do upon release, William said with a smile that he wants to "go on a week's vacation and soak in Epsom salt." He made it clear that, although it is an easy thing to fall back into and he is unsure of his ability not to, selling drugs is not what he wants to do with the rest of his life because "losing family and freedom, isn't worth it."

For William, the distance in his relationship with his mother compelled some of the choices he made in life. Particularly, her absence seemed to influence his drug use and, ultimately, his decision to sell drugs full time. Similarly, William's love for his stepdaughters affects the decisions he will make once released. Clearly, the individuals most important to these inmates play a significant role in their past decisions and future possibilities. Yet, the 'Pathway to Change' program insists on framing the influence of family and friends as either supportive or unsupportive and constructs these important relationships in unrealistic characterizations.

These typical cognitive restructuring exercises provide a useful tool for encouraging self-analysis. But, in a limited environment like a prison, devoid of context and real-world applicability, these questions are simply interesting things to think about, not behavior-changing life-skills the inmates can use when they get out.

The major failure of the 'Pathway to Change' program is truly represented here; it starts the inmates down the path to cognitive self-change, but it abandons them part of the way there. The program's lack of personalization, explanation and follow-through not only make it incomplete, but also make it potentially dangerous for the inmates. If they're given tools without the training to know how to use them in the real world, they could easily misinterpret whatever knowledge they may have gained in the program and find themselves, instead, more confused than they were before.

Yet, it was clear during my interviews with the inmates that many of them had begun to consider some of the tools the program emphasized. The language they use is similar to the language in the manual, though whether they were simply saying what they thought I wanted to hear or whether they had truly begun to understand those tools is debatable. Steven, a twenty-seven-year-old Black man from a large urban area, gives us an example. Steven is addicted to heroin and has used alcohol, cocaine, marijuana and PCP. He has three children.

Steven said his neighborhood growing up was very rough because "everything you can name" was going on there. He lived with his mother and father and seven siblings. His dad worked in a food factory and his mother stayed home. The most important person to him growing up was his little sister and the most important people to him now are his three children. Steven is in prison for violating his parole on a previous charge.

I asked Steven why he believes he is in prison and he replied: "probably just my time to come. Can't blame nobody but myself." I asked him if he believed he would ever come back and he said: "I pray to God that I don't." Steven wants to own his own lawn care business and be a good father. I asked what advice he would give to others like himself and he replied: "tell them my life story. The first thing I gotta do is work on my thoughts. I have to sit down and actually think about the consequences."

Steven's words are a direct reflection of the messages provided in the 'Pathway to Change' program. Working on one's thoughts and considering the consequences of one's actions before engaging in those actions are typical cognitive-behavioral exercises and, it would seem, Steven understands that considering consequences is an essential element to eventually changing his behaviors. He also reflects the program's tenets by stating that the blame for his current incarceration rests solely on himself. Earlier, the self-blame ideology was discussed at length as one of the primary principles of the program. But Steven also stated that it may have just been his time to come to prison and he prays he won't come back. This attention toward forces beyond his control also indicates that Steven does not fully believe that the things he learned in the program, such as working on his thoughts or considering consequences, are all there is to staying out of prison. The program here is clearly incomplete in its linkage of the principles of cognitive-behavioral therapies to their empirical application. Thus, Steven is left with some helpful tools, but no knowledge whatsoever of how to realistically use them.

We see further evidence of these contextual voids in Lesson 9 "You Can Control Your Thoughts" (19–20). The stated objective is "to help participants understand the effect of tragic thinking on the decision-making process." The lesson prompts the instructor to play different selections of music from different styles and genres and have the members of the class write down on slips of paper how each selection made them feel. The instructor is to repeat this process with several different musical selections then break the class into as many groups as there were selections played. Each group represents a particular selection; the groups are instructed to read the slips of paper collected from the class that go with their selection and create a skit that embodies the various feelings written on the paper about the music selection. The manual encourages the instructor to have each group perform their skit in front of the class and play the music selection in the background. The lesson concludes by introducing the "secrets" to controlling one's thoughts. These secrets include statements like: "your mind can only think of one thing at a time," and "thoughts lead to actions sooner or later," so participants ought to simply choose to think of positive things and, therefore, positive actions will follow.

Again, the program provides a set of "skills," but neglects to also provide direction or connection to the elements of the lesson itself or to any actual situation where the inmates can use the skills they learned. The failure of this lesson to adequately explain how different genres of music in any way relate to the questions the inmates were asked, as well as how any of it matters in the real world, is baffling. Further, the connection between the inmates being forced to perform musical theater and how they can better control their thoughts is entirely lost. It is difficult to understand what possible connection there could be between the inmates dancing and acting out skits about their feelings to background music in front of an audience of guards and other inmates with how they can learn to make better decisions based on changing their thinking patterns from a negative state to a positive one. The connection (if there is any) is not explained, either explicitly or implicitly and, again, the inmates are left to wonder and struggle on their own.

Chad's struggle with this very concept is exemplified in his story. Chad is a twenty-four-year-old Black man from the inner city of a large urban area. Chad grew up living with his mother because his parents were divorced. His mother was "a caregiver for the mentally challenged" and his father was "a drug dealer and Realtor." Chad said the most important person in his life when he was growing up was his little brother because "he reminded me of myself." Chad's little brother is now serving out a life sentence in prison for murder. Chad said as a teenager he "sold heroin and ecstasy and used crack as another form of currency." Chad is single and has one daughter who is nine years old.

At seventeen years old, Chad received five years of supervised probation for being in possession of a stolen car. At nineteen, Chad violated his probation by being in possession of drugs and received a one-year prison sentence. He violated his parole and is currently serving two more years in prison; Chad is scheduled for release in three months.

I asked Chad who or what was the main reason for his current incarceration and he replied: "I put myself in a certain environment. I didn't have to stay on that side of town. I was addicted to it, but it's a cat and mouse game. I know I contradict myself." I asked him, finally, what advice he would give to other people in his position and he said: "you learn: once you keep your hands clean – you stay out of trouble. Everything comes with a price."

Lesson 9 claims to be able to provide the inmates with the "secrets" to controlling their thoughts. As a participant in the program, however, Chad seems flummoxed by his own realization that while he is responsible for controlling his thoughts and actions, he cannot realistically manage those thoughts and actions in the environment where he lives. Chad's acknowledgment that his statements about controlling his thoughts and his addiction to the lifestyle are contradictory illustrates the intense feelings of confusion and frustration experienced by many of the men participating in this program. The manual neglects to explain exactly how the inmates should connect their thoughts to their actions. The result is that they're left confused and directionless.

Lesson 9 also gives rise to one of the most persistent themes in the manual, which is also the basic agenda of the state: expert knowledge. The production of expert knowledge is evident in the way the 'secrets to positive thinking' provided in the lesson are presented as an unquestionable reality. There is no place for the discussion or debate of these "secrets," nor is there any evidence provided that speaks to their accuracy. Is it true that our minds can only think of one thing at a time, or that all thoughts eventually lead to actions? The inmates are simply given the information, told to believe it and blamed when things don't turn out the way they expected. Dictating expert knowledge in this way ignores a basic element of social life: it's unpredictability. Such definitive statements are not framed as suggestions for how to control one's thoughts, but touted as so many mystical secrets that, once imbued upon them, the inmates should have no trouble adopting.

Expert knowledge

In addition to the ideas of self-blame and degradation as tools to changing inmates' thinking patterns, and the disconnections between the objectives and methods used in the lessons as well as their detachment from reality, we also see the theme of expert knowledge begin to take shape. Previously, I defined *expert knowledge* as the unquestioned institutional meta-narrative espoused by policy makers, administrators, practitioners and scholars to inform policies and programs. Within the 'Pathway to Change' program itself and throughout the individual lessons, expert knowledge presents itself primarily through converting broad-based, philosophical ideas into over-simplified, universal standards. Most problematic here is that the definitions provided for these ideas are offered without qualification and are presented definitively. The heavy-handed presentation of concepts sets up expert knowledge as unquestionable and asserts that the inmates must accept these definitions as the truth. The inclusion of answer keys within each lesson also speaks to how expert knowledge creates an incontestable discursive framework from which the inmates ought not deviate.

In Lesson 3, the unquestionable presence of expert knowledge takes shape in the form of opinion statements touted as absolute reality (7–8). The stated objective is "to allow participants to see the affect [sic] that their environment has on their decisions" and then to help them see that they can overcome that environment. First, the teacher is instructed to have everyone in the class pick out a random item from a bag (the manual simply suggests filling the bag with "interesting" objects) and go around the room so each inmate can share a situation they have had involving the item.

Next, the manual instructs the teacher to define the words "fate," "nature," and "nurture" in the following ways; *fate* "is the situation and elements of your birth. These are things about yourself that you cannot change." For instance, the manual suggests, things like height, skin color and gender are elements of fate. Next, the manual defines *nature* as "all the things a person likes to do. These are the things about yourself that you can change." It suggests that career choices, favorite foods and the presence of significant others are elements of one's nature. Finally, the concept of *nurture* is defined as "the way you were raised. It includes all of the environmental factors you experienced while you were growing up. These are things about yourself that you can also change (8)."

The instructor should then provide the group with sets of 3×5 cards with different words written on them. The inmates decide whether the word on the card is best related to fate, nature or nurture. Some suggestions for words to put on the cards include things like favorite food or movies, family traditions, pant size, religion, envy, parents, morals and neighborhood.

The 'Pathway to Change' author provided his opinion regarding the elements comprising the socially constructed concepts of fate, nature and nurture. The Missouri Department of Corrections accepted his definitions as adequate and provided them to the inmates as fact. The presentation of these definitions, given to the inmates as definitive, real and absolute, embodies the production and transmission of *expert knowledge*. When a person (or program, policy, lesson, manual, instructor, institution, state, etc.) in a position of power provides a piece of knowledge or information to an individual who is in a fully subordinate position, then that knowledge is immediately indisputable. The very idea that any one person can define concepts like fate, nature and nurture (or that these concepts are definable at all) supports the disciplinary rhetoric of the type of expert knowledge that is forced upon, and ultimately comes to define, the inmates' individual experiences. Indeed, cognitive self-change programs encourage a change in thinking patterns and these definitions provided to the inmates may very well accomplish the goal. Yet, the definitions are provided based on someone else's reality, not the inmates'. They don't come to these ideas, definitions or conclusions on their own; they are fed them via the opinions of "experts." Unable to debate or even question the validity of these definitions, inmates may change their thinking patterns (or at least attempt to) at the cost of giving up their ability to think critically on their own altogether. Add to the production of expert knowledge the disconnectedness of pulling something from "the bag of interesting items" as well as the humiliating experience of being forced to manipulate other inmates' bodies to create a "living sculpture" depicting the inadequacies of their family members, and we see that the program continues to move farther away from addressing any of the inmates' potential problems in a realistic way.

The problem of defining ideas like fate, nature and nurture as static and unquestionable concepts is apparent in Dan's story. Dan is a White male, twenty-four years old and from a mid-sized city in the southern Midwest. Dan has served most of his life in correctional facilities. He dropped out of school in the eleventh grade but wants to go back for his bachelor's degree in accounting or business. His parents are divorced so he grew up living with his mother. She worked as an exotic dancer and Dan's father was a truck driver and tattoo artist. Dan said that just about everyone he knows has been to prison, mostly for charges related to methamphetamine. Dan said the most important person in his life as a child was his mother because he could talk to her about anything. The most important person to him now is his six-year-old son. Dan's parents split when he was twenty-two because his father beat Dan's mother. Dan is currently separated from his wife but is in a relationship with a forty-year-old woman whom he met while getting high with her son.

Dan's first encounter with the law was when he was fourteen years old after he stabbed another boy at school. Dan was sent to "boot camp" until he was seventeen years old. At seventeen, he was on probation but violated it and was then sent to a "trade school" where he stayed until he was twenty-one. Dan said the first time he did drugs he was ten years old and he snorted some cocaine his mother had left lying on the coffee table. Dan has done drugs ever since.

The first time Dan served a sentence in an adult correctional facility he was twenty-two years old and was convicted of passing bad checks and violating his probation. He was released but soon caught with an unlicensed .45 caliber handgun and (as a violation of his probation) he did 120 days in prison. Dan said that he currently owns 212 guns and believes himself to be an accomplished collector. While on probation, Dan was pulled over while driving and was caught with the same gun and sentenced to seven years in prison. He has served eight months and will be released in eighteen days. He will be on probation until the year 2015. After his release, Dan plans to move to a "ranch out west" to complete a one-year "after-care" program and engage in faith-based activities such as attending church once per week and paying the ranch eighty dollars per week plus two hours of maintenance work.

I asked Dan how he could avoid coming back to prison and he replied: "to be honest, I won't know till I get out." I asked Dan who or what was the primary reason for his current incarceration and he said: "I chose to do everything I've done. It was fun at the time." I then asked him if he believed having been caught with the same unlicensed gun twice in a row was a choice and he replied: "no, that's just nature."

Dan's version of "nature" includes owning guns and the inevitability of being caught with them. He seemed to accept his lot in life from growing up with drug addicted parents in poverty while also acknowledging his own efforts in coming to prison. Dan seems to have internalized at least some of the cognitive self-change rhetoric by admitting that his own choices landed him in prison, but he maintains that carrying unlicensed firearms and being caught with them is natural and thus, presumably, out of his control. The program's lack of specificity in defining concepts like fate, nature and nurture is problematic because Dan clearly has preexisting notions of these concepts but is forbidden from incorporating any life experience into their definition. Expert knowledge in this sense lacks the evidence necessary to back up its claims. As a result, inmates are given information inconsistent with their own experiences and no guidance to help reconcile the differences.

A most compelling example of the contradictory relationship between the concepts in the program and the experienced lives of the inmates appears in Ed's story. Ed is twenty-six, White and from a mid-sized town in the Midwest.

He dropped out of high school in the tenth grade and is currently taking classes toward the completion of his GED. He said the first time he did drugs he was fifteen years old and smoked marijuana with his older brother. Since then, he has done cocaine, crack and meth. Ed is currently in prison for the third time.

Ed was raised by his mother and had no relationship with his father because he died when Ed was young. Ed has five siblings, four of whom have also been to jail. Ed's mother worked in a morgue and at gas stations to support him and his siblings. Growing up, the most important person in Ed's life was his grandmother because, he said, she spoiled him. Now, the most important person in his life is his mother because she has always been there for him. Ed has never been married and has no children.

Ed first got in trouble when he was twenty years old. He and a friend kicked in the window of a storefront and stole electronics and money from the cash register. They hid the stolen goods in the woods until they could find someone to sell them to. When they went back to the woods to get the stolen property, they were seen by a police officer and were arrested. Ed went to prison for 120 days. Shortly after his release he violated his parole by failing a drug test. He did another twenty-one months in prison and stayed clean for three months following his release. Ed said he did roofing jobs and began to make money but soon started drinking and doing cocaine. He lost his job, his sister kicked him out of her house and he got drunk and tried to walk into a house that wasn't his. He was convicted of attempting to enter a residence and was sent back to prison. Ed did five months in the county jail, three months in another state prison and has done sixteen months in the current institution. He will be out in two weeks and will have to serve two months of house arrest and two years on parole.

I asked Ed why he believed he was in prison right now and he replied: "I got mixed up with some female, but it was my own fault. If I would have made the right choice I wouldn't be here. I'll go talk to my mom if I need help." Finally, I asked Ed if he believed he would ever come back to prison. He replied: "I'm gonna do my best to stay out." Ed wants to enlist in the Marines or the Army because, he said: "if I did something like that, I'd get the discipline I didn't get growing up."

It is quite insightful for Ed to recognize that his childhood and adolescence lacked discipline. After his father died, Ed's mother worked to support her children. However, despite her efforts, five of her six children have served time in jail or prison. Ed seems to realize that there were things in his upbringing influencing the actions that led him to prison. According to the 'Pathway to Change' program, however, nurture (or the way one was raised including values and prejudices) is something that can be changed.

The expert knowledge provided by the prison in the form of this program alleges that an individual has the ability to change the way they were raised, which can determine their values, prejudices and attitudes. The program conflates "all of the environmental factors" one experiences during childhood with personal viewpoints. Though related, these things are not the same. The program neglects to acknowledge that socialization (or "nurture") is a lifelong process. In the same way it neglected to recognize that the "problem" people in an inmate's life are also the people with whom he often feels the strongest bonds, the program ignores the fact that adults continue to learn from their environments and that their environments consist of people who share their world-views.

By telling the inmates that they can change both nature and nurture without explaining exactly how they should go about it, the program sets them up to fail. The expert knowledge espoused here provides incomplete and inadequate definitions of highly complex, socially constructed concepts and tells the inmates that the power to change them is all in their hands. Using these definitions of fate, nature and nurture, few people could successfully make the changes that the program prescribes. For Brian, the frustration with knowing what to do but not being able to do it has given way to despondence.

Brian is a twenty-three-year-old Black man from the inner city of a large midwestern city. He dropped out of high school in the eleventh grade but wants to go back to school someday and get his bachelor's degree. Brian said the area where he lived with his mother and stepfather was a rough place with drugs and guns. He has two older brothers, both of whom have also been to prison. Brian's step-dad worked as a janitor in the high school where Brian went. He lived with his grandparents for a time growing up and he said they were the most important people in his life at the time. Now, Brian says, the most important person in his life is his step-dad because he's always been there for him. Brian has a three-year-old daughter with his girlfriend.

Brian began getting in trouble as a teenager but received his first prison sentence in his early twenties. He and some friends stole a car and began a high-speed chase when a police officer tried to pull them over. The police threw down a spike strip and stopped the car but Brian got out and ran. He was caught by the police and sat in the county jail for a year before being sentenced to four years in prison. All but six months of those four years were considered time served.

Brian violated his parole by not reporting to his parole officer and was sentenced to another six months in prison. He was to be released in a month, as of the time of this writing. I asked Brian why he ran from the police when he was caught with the stolen car and he replied: "I didn't feel like giving up. I know now you might as well give up." I asked Brian why he believes he is currently incarcerated and he said: "myself – because I know I have a lot of sense; what to do and what not to do. I blame myself for being in this situation." Brian plans to "start working, stop hanging around the wrong crowd and think about the people who love you" when he gets out. I asked Brian what advice he would give to others like himself and he replied: "prison ain't fun so find a job, go back to school. Live your life right, don't live the street life." Finally, I asked Brian if he believed he would ever be back in prison. He said: "depends on when I get out – how I see myself."

For Brian, the expert definitions of fate, nature and nurture leave him with little recourse in dealing with the events of his life. If Brian believed that he could change his nature and nurture, it is doubtful that his ultimate perspective on life would involve "giving up." If one could truly change nature and nurture, it is expected that the inmates' stories would include significantly more optimism for the future than they do. The program gives them false hope in its unrealistic definitions of these concepts. The individualization of nature and nurture here grossly misinterprets empirical constraints on the possibility of enacting change and, so, rather than failing again, the inmates simply stop trying altogether.

Brian, though, is not alone in his despondence. Alex, a twenty-two-year-old Black man from the inner city area of a large metropolis shares in Brian's conclusion to "give up." Alex dropped out of high school in the eleventh grade but now regrets that decision. He plans on continuing his education and wants to go to a community college to major in zoology. When Alex was thirteen years old he first witnessed some people in the neighborhood doing drugs. He tried marijuana for the first time when he was fourteen and has since done heroin and PCP.

Alex said the area where he lived was very rough and he became a member of a prominent gang. His father left when Alex was twelve and his mother remarried. Alex's mom worked at a pet food factory and his dad was employed by the city. The most important person in his life was, and still is, his mother because she has always been there for him. Alex is single and has no children. He is currently serving time in prison for the unlawful use of a weapon and possession of heroin.

The first time Alex got in trouble was when he was twenty-one years old. He was pulled over for driving with a broken taillight and the officer found heroin in the glove box, a gun in the backseat and ecstasy pills in Alex's pocket. Alex received five years' probation but violated his probation by not reporting to his probation officer. He was arrested and served one year in prison. After his release, Alex needed money and said his friend convinced him to rob houses. The two were caught and arrested and Alex received his current sentence, on which he has served one year. I asked Alex why he thought he was in prison today and he answered: "I blame my homeboy. I shoulda not helped this guy but you know, you kind of give up." I asked him what he thought he could do to stay out of prison for a third time and he replied: "there's only one way; you gotta be civilized." Finally, I asked Alex if he believed he would ever be back in prison. He answered: "yes. I aint found myself yet."

For both Alex and Brian, the thought of simply "giving up" resonates. Both of these recidivists indicate that the conditions in their lives made them feel powerless to fight against them. Thus, "giving up" for Brian and Alex essentially means "giving in" to the pressures of life on the street and, almost inevitably, also to the reality of doing time in prison.

The lessons in the 'Pathway to Change' manual all rest on this basic foundation of expert knowledge. The fact that the manual provides correct answers to completely subjective questions throughout the program inherently limits the potential of this program to work successfully on any one individual. Because the program is standardized and premised upon a one-size-fits-all framework, it is entirely inevitable that some of the inmates will fall through the cracks in the program. This resolution would remain a neutral outcome if the inmates simply received no help from the program. However, the reality of these lessons is that they do not just provide inadequate aid to the inmates, but they also have the potential to become the direct and proximate cause of harm to the well-being of the inmates forced to participate. By virtue of being forced to participate, the inmates have no choice but to engage in whatever degrading or humiliating activity the instructor dictates. Ironically, the program's basis that "there is always a choice in one's behavior" is truly put to the test as it effectively forces the principles of expert knowledge onto the inmates and sets up their re-articulation as a condition of release.

Understanding the power dynamics at play in this program, it is no wonder that many of the inmates' stories articulate (and contradict) the principles of 'Pathway to Change.' However, in many of the stories their resistance to the program's expert knowledge is also evident. Take, for instance, Derek, a twenty-six-year-old White man from a large city in the Midwest. He was kicked out of school in the twelfth grade but has since received his GED. He is currently enrolled in a community college that starts a few weeks after he is scheduled for release. Derek wants to get his bachelor's degree in drafting design. Derek says he is addicted to cocaine and methamphetamine.

Derek said he lived in a rough neighborhood growing up because there were drugs and robbery. Both his parents dropped out of high school and his father is currently in prison. His dad worked as a mechanic and his mother stayed at home. Derek is single and has a six-year-old son. Derek's first run-in with the law happened when he was eighteen and he and some friends stole a car, leading the police in a high-speed chase. Derek said: "that's just what everybody did in that area – stole cars; it was a rush." Derek received 120 days in prison and five years of probation. At twenty-two he violated his probation by failing a drug test and he went on the run. He was caught with cocaine in a rental car while on the run and was sentenced to three years in prison. Derek said of his incarceration: "it's my own fault. Every move I make, my eyes are open. I know the consequences of all my actions." I asked if prison has taught him anything and he replied: "no, it's all common sense. The only thing that's gonna stop me from breaking the law is when I'm done doing it. I can't even say for sure I'm not coming back. I hope to God I don't come back. If I can get out and make it till August eighteenth, I'm good." Classes started at the community college, where Derek was enrolled, on that date.

For Derek, the key to staying out of prison is common sense. He resists the imposition of expert knowledge from the prison and yet simultaneously embraces one of its basic principles: the choice/blame ideology. For Derek, the only thing that can prevent him from coming back to prison is himself, although he is entirely unsure whether or not he will come back. This confusion and contradiction is characteristic of so many of the stories from the men taking this class. It is evident that many of them want to change, and may even have been hopeful about their chances at the beginning of the program, but most of them eventually gave in to the realization that the 'Pathway to Change' program held nothing of real value to them. The lessons, activities and advice in the program were the knowledge of experts, not the reality of their lives. Harold perhaps articulates this problem best of all: Harold is a thirty-two-year-old Black and Native American man from a large city in the Midwest. He dropped out of school because he had to go to work to help his family. He has received his GED and plans to go to school for an associate's degree in business. Harold is addicted to PCP.

Growing up, Harold lived with his mother and stepfather, three younger sisters, three half-brothers and a stepsister. His mother was a court stenographer and his dad worked for a large airline company. The most important person in his life growing up was his uncle because he was a "supportive father figure." Now, the most important person in Harold's life is his two-year-old son because Harold believes that he "needs to break this chain."

Harold was sent to prison the first time when he was twenty-four years old and was arrested for the possession of crack for sale. He did two-and-a-half years in prison but violated his parole by not completing substance abuse classes. He has been in prison now for a year and he says he hopes this is his last time. I asked him why he thought he was in prison today and Harold said: "time is the most valuable thing I got to offer and if I'm sitting in here I got nothing to offer nobody. It all boils down to choice." I asked what, if anything, prison had taught him and Harold replied:

> the more productive classes help with resumes and checkbooks and job interviews. But the other ones – they take the classes out of context of real life. They say they're giving us the tools to live, but experience is the best teacher. It'd be nice to see ex-offenders run those types of programs. Just share how they took the first step. The most successful programs on the outside have to do with ex-offenders. You can't teach life out of a book.

References

Foucault, M. (1979). *Discipline and punish: The birth of the prison*. New York: Second Vintage Books.

Henry, S. & Milovanovic, D. (1996). *Constitutive criminology: Beyond postmodernism*. Thousand Oaks, CA: Sage Publications.

'Pathway to Change'. (2005). *Introductory manual*. Clime International.

Reiman, J. (2009). The moral ambivalence of crime in an unjust society. In J. Reiman and P. Leighton (Eds.), *The rich get richer and the poor get prison: A reader*. New York: Pearson.

8 Crossing over

"Probably just my time to come. Can't blame nobody but myself."

Steven, 27

Common and disparate patterns revealed in five themes

Throughout this book I have provided my critique of the mandatory 'Pathway to Change' program within the context of the storied lives of the inmates I interviewed. Each interviewee had either taken, or was currently enrolled in, the program and it is important to tie their words as closely as possible to the material from the manual in order to effectively ground the resulting analyses and critiques. My critiques are rooted in the empirical data gathered from both "sides" of the fence: the expert knowledge of the prison and Department of Corrections and the often similar and always contradictory lived realities of the inmates.

In addition to examining the empirical data in the case presented here, tying the mechanics and consequences of discursive discipline to broad, cultural expectations of acceptable language and personal storytelling is similarly important. To do this, I identify five underlying patterns emergent from all the data sets examined here. These five themes; choice, responsibility, goals, context and future, are common across every individual story, each Department of Corrections statement or policy and in every lesson of the program. The themes summarize the primary foci of the state and the individuals it controls, and link, even more closely, the guiding thread that both mutually connects and simultaneously confounds the relationship of the inmates to the meta-narrative of the state. These themes, however, can also be found in the language of our broader cultural dialogues. It will be shown in this chapter, first, how the five themes persist across all of the empirical data sets, highlighting their interconnections and constituting the impossibility of their separation from one another. These threads weave the individuals' stories tightly into the fabric of the institutional story, strengthening the bonds that tether them to both the prison and to similar meta-narratives in the greater cultural milieu. Second, the examination of these themes will illustrate their discursive power as ultimate and effective disciplinary techniques. The application of these ideas by the state onto individuals through rhetoric and coercion defines the subtle and seemingly benign nature of their use as tools of social control. These themes, found in policies and programs, are the invisible bars of institutional and social regulation. They are the panoptic, regulatory and indisputable forces of discursive discipline, crafted by expert knowledge and, therefore, unquestionably relevant.

The five themes discussed here are planted into the thoughts, words and rewritten histories of the inmates. Eventually, they will be released from the physical confines of the prison, but they'll take with them these ideas, rooted into how they are able to think, speak and understand themselves and the world around them. Their freedom outside of prison then becomes, in many ways, as confining and regulated as their lives inside prison. Discipline is no longer restricted to their physical incarceration, but is embedded in their available discourses, personal vocabularies and conceptions of themselves. In this way, the inmates' physical freedom is not without a price. In order to earn that physical freedom, they were coerced into adopting the language of the institutional meta-narrative; failure to do so, they knew, would result in further physical confinement. Like most of us probably would, they acquiesced in order to earn their freedom. The cost, however, is higher than they likely imagined.

Freedom, for these men, is a concept that is both fluid in its definition and at the same time rigid in its application. Practically, the idea of being "free" is equated to being physically released from the confines of prison walls and the omnipresent gaze of regulatory agents. Discursively, however, freedom for inmates is a much less tangible notion. They were coerced into learning about and, at least outwardly, adopting the language of the institutional and larger cultural meta-narratives. Adopting the language of the experts likely served as a means to an end for many of the inmates as it was the currency by which they were able to buy their physical freedom. However, what they may not realize is that in the process of bartering for their release from prison, their personal, lived, experienced histories, the truth behind the reasons for their actions and the reality of their struggles on the outside were devalued, deleted and replaced with the same stories and truths that every other law-abiding citizen is expected to proclaim.

Whether or not the inmates simply say what they need to say in order to get out of prison, or if they truly embody their newly acquired discourses, is wholly irrelevant. What matters is that there is one single narrative they are all expected to embrace; failure to do so inside the prison results in their continued incarceration. Failure to do so outside of prison results in the same potential consequence that it does for every other "free" citizen: social rejection.

Theme one: choice

One of the first sentences in the introduction to the 'Pathway to Change' manual reads, "even when things happen that are out of your control, you always have the ability to choose how you will deal with the situation." Taking this statement as a definitive explanation for the starting point of the class as it pertains to employing the cognitive self-change agenda, I find that all thirty of the inmates expressed this sentiment in one form or another during our interview. The idea of "there always being a choice" is a persistent theme in both 'Pathway to Change' and the inmates' narratives. I do not assume that the choice component in the inmates' narratives necessarily sprung from their participation in the class, though this is likely the case for many. The choice theme persists in each man's story as it does in the rhetoric of the program. Here, we see the inmates' awareness of the "choice" ideologies as they have integrated them into their stories:

SAM: I coulda changed – I chose to live this life. Maybe it's 'cause I wasn't trying to break the cycle.

WAYNE: You gotta make your own choices and take it for what it is. I've made a lot of stupid choices and I'll make a lot more but I wouldn't have changed anything I've done.

DAN: I chose to do everything I've done.

ED: If I would have made the right choice I wouldn't be here.

HAROLD: It all boils down to choice.

The "choice" theme is one of the most prevalent and persistent across each data set. The inmates' narratives match this theme in almost every case. From the lessons themselves, the "choice" theme can be found throughout the workbook but most prominently appears in Lesson 12: "Decisions." The offenders are asked to solve a variety of problems. A few of the problems the workbook suggests include greedy astronauts in a space capsule eating too much food, a married couple struggling with making the decision on which car to purchase and the warden of a prison lacking enough room for a group of incoming inmates. The 'Pathway to Change' workbook uses these hypothetical scenarios to illustrate the idea that "there is always a choice." But, a married couple trying to decide which car to buy represents a heteronormative, white, middle class "problem" that (in comparison with the inmates' life stories) is hardly a relevant example of a problem that would be difficult to solve. We know from mainstream media representations in advertising that the couples agonizing over the decision to purchase a Lexus or an Escalade are almost always depicted as white, heterosexual, married and financially stable. Their struggle is often characterized such that their decisions rest on things like determining which car gets the better gas mileage, not whether they can afford a car at all. In an example indicating that the couple had only a little money saved up and had to choose between buying a car so they could make it to work on time and using the money to buy their children winter clothing, the choice would be more reflective of the narratives the offenders live out daily. Using the hypothetical example of astronauts in space eating too much food is, again, an irrelevant example in the context of the audience. A problem asking the offenders to make a choice between allowing their brother who had recently become homeless to come and live with them when they do not have the extra room or money for food would make the program's insistence that there is always a choice seem more pertinent. In each case, considering the social histories and environmental contexts the inmates come from and will return to is a concept that is almost entirely neglected in 'Pathway to Change.'

The inmates required to participate in 'Pathway to Change' are those being transitioned from prison back into the community. They will all be released within months of their completion of the class. It seems that hypothetical examples about astronauts may not accurately reflect any sort of problems the individuals in prison will face the day they walk out. Deciding which car to purchase likely seems moot if the inmates are struggling with the knowledge that the day they are released from prison they will have no reliable form of transportation just to get back to the temporary, if stable, residence they were required to list in their release papers.

The Missouri Reentry Process *Strategic Plan* makes the claim that "the ultimate goal is to produce an 'employable offender.' All areas of education must overlap and share, teaching functional concepts" (Missouri Department of Corrections, 2009b). The functionality of concepts teaching the offenders how to make decisions is neglected in 'Pathway to Change.' It may be the case that other classes offered at state prisons teach functional, realistic skills and tools for success, but in 'Pathway to Change' the overlap does not exist. In the case of 'Pathway to Change,' the idea that "there is always a choice" is being taught with methods that do not take the target audience into consideration at all. Thought exercises are interesting ways to get individuals to become self-reflective and consider their own decision making processes; but the examples used to encourage these thought exercises are far from functional when the contextual realities of the inmates' lives both inside and outside of prison are considered.

As is evident from the data, the "choice" theme the Department of Corrections supports is present both in the inmates' narratives and the 'Pathway to Change' class. The inmates all made statements that reflected the Department of Corrections meta-narrative that "there is always a choice." They have incorporated this piece of the cognitive self-change agenda into their personal narratives, on some level or another. Whether the inmates have truly internalized it is here unknowable and largely irrelevant, but the data strongly reflect their acknowledgment and incorporation of the "choice" ideology into the words they use to describe themselves and their life chances. Thus, the inmates' narratives indicate they have learned that they can always make choices but they continue to express confusion in precisely how to make *better* choices.

The choice problem

The idea that "there is always a choice" is not unique to 'Pathway to Change,' the prison or the state; it is a common theme that persists in our current cultural environment. Rational-choice theory, in particular, embraces and argues that actors consistently, and thus also rationally, choose to engage in behaviors that are of most benefit (utility) to them (Sugden, 1991). In this way, the theory posits that we can then use the patterned behaviors of individuals' choices to make predictions about their future actions. For Sugden, "any *theory* of choice must postulate some consistent pattern be found in people's rational choices and then anyone who chooses as the theory predicts must be acting consistently with that pattern and therefore rationally" (1991; 752). For Sugden, the problem with conventional rational-choice theory is that it assumes that all agents have the same *type* of rationality, whereas in actuality different people exhibit and employ various types of rationality based on any number of subjective criteria. For instance, he argues for two particular types of rational actors: the *resolute* person and the *forward-looking* person (780–1). The resolute type of rationality assumes that the individual in question makes his or her plans with full intent to carry them out, without reconsidering them over the course of time, save an unforeseen, intervening event. Resolute rationalists believe that whatever plans they made originally will still be valid and utilitarian at a future point in time and, thus, *resolve* to carry them out. Their actions, then, can be easily predicted if the predictor understands that they are a resolute actor. All of their future behaviors will be directed toward fulfilling their original goal.

Forward-looking rationalists use prior information and knowledge they believe they will gain in the future to appraise a stance that they take on an issue when it becomes useful to do so, not just in the face of an unforeseen intervening event. So they are less committed to their original position, but more able to see how making a statement now can rationally benefit them, when their intent may be to change their position on that statement all along. Forward-looking rationalists know that it would benefit them more to *make* a claim in the present, but perhaps not to truly *act* on it in the future. So if the forward-looking rationalist deems it to be beneficial to adopt a resolute rationality in the moment, he or she does so with the knowledge that they are simply *acting* resolutely, but all the time maintaining a *forward-looking* position. The forward-looking rationalist is no less honest than the resolute rationalist, as both types of individuals direct their action toward the most utilitarian end. Conventional rational-choice theory, however, is less able to predict the future actions and potentialities of the forward-looking individual and, thus, the less predictable his or her choices are, the more utilitarian they become.

It can be said that there is "always a choice." The consequences, however, may be equally negative to whomever is deciding between them. So, the real problem then becomes in determining which type of rationality the individual employs to decide which very negative outcome to choose. Our current cultural meta-narrative suggests that we should all claim and strive to be resolute rationalists; that commitment, consistency, resolve and dedication to our choices and actions is commendable (King, 1988). We believe someone to be admirable when they make a decision and stick with it, despite opportunities to abandon the original resolution in favor of a previously unforeseen, more favorable outcome. We use turns of phrase that promote resolute rationality such as: “honesty is the best policy,” or “stick to your guns” or “stand your ground.” We encourage children to always tell the truth, to stand up for what they believe in and to always do the right thing. We use these ideals as standards for good living and praise those who embody them. And so, it is built into the language of our culture that there is always the opportunity to choose between good and bad or right and wrong, even at the cost of our own comfort or better judgment. The problem, of course, is that most of us aren’t resolute rationalists but, rather, forward-looking individuals who understand the inherent unpredictability of life and, therefore, take care to make our daily choices as unbounded as possible. We never hear people say: “do the right thing … unless something more benefiting to you comes along,” and yet that is what most of us tend to do whether or not we’d like to admit it.

The master meta-narrative of our contemporary culture is based on irrational, though highly utilitarian, principles. In prison, these principles are touted as the keys to life and that if the inmates can just come around to the idea that there is always a choice (in the practical sense) and that they should just consistently choose the “right” one, then they will be successful. “Right” in this sense means always following the law and, as a resolute rationalist, it makes sense to commit to always following the law. But, as freethinking, forward-looking people the inmates are aware that time, space and circumstance are changeable and uncontrollable and that to survive in such an environment requires the ability to assess and reevaluate previously decided-upon paths of action and, sometimes, to change one’s mind.

Forward-looking rationality and resolute rationality represent a cultural binary. One makes sense given the innumerable probabilities for action and circumstance taken into account when other actors and institutions are introduced into a person’s environment. The other makes sense in a world where things feel safer and make more sense when people’s actions can be easily predicted.

When the institutional meta-narrative reflects the cultural meta-narrative about choosing to do the right thing, the inmates are, again, coerced into adopting a stance on their lives that is inconsistent with their past experiences and knowledge about what the future holds for them. The problem, they’re told, is with them. They are made to believe that their inability or resistance to adopt a resolute type of rationality means that there is a flaw in their thinking patterns. The larger, more pervasive problem, however, is that the focus is on their personal failings, rather than on the weaknesses of a system of rationalizing that is subjectively impractical for anyone, let alone prison inmates.

Discursive discipline is enacted here, as well. The cognitive self-change ideology promotes resolute rationality as the standard, universally applicable method for personal decision making. In telling the inmates that the reason they are in prison is because of their bad choices and the way to stay out of prison is to stop making bad choices, the subjective individual reasons for those original choices become swallowed up by the new idea they're told to adopt: that good citizens always make the good decision to follow the law. And so, it makes sense: if one wants to stay out of prison, one should simply be resolute in not breaking the law. In this way, the inmates are punished twofold. First, if they simply refuse to engage the program and its ideologies, they are punished with confinement. Second, if they agree to use a resolute system of rational decision making they should be able to easily predict the outcomes of their future actions and stay out of prison; however, they are destined to fail when, inevitably, they revert to the much more utilitarian and practical forward-looking rationality that allows them to survive in dynamic environments.

There is always a choice in one's behavior, according to the prison program. Indeed, this can be taken as a truth. But, when that statement is used as a proxy for real, tangible solutions that could actually be used in tough, dynamic situations simply because resolute rationality is predictable and, thus, its users more controllable, the effects are like sending these inmates out into a warzone without proper armor, training or even the permission to change their minds when it might be most beneficial for them to do so.

Theme two: responsibility

The notion of making choices and the idea of being responsible for the consequences of those choices, are inextricably linked. When a person makes a choice (which we have here discovered that the state believes is always possible), it follows that, in making that "rational" choice, the actor thus takes responsibility for whatever outcomes result because of the choice. Taking responsibility then is also considered (at least systemically and culturally) as a rational act, deemed a necessary evil of the result of rational choosing. It is further understood that a person who is to be held responsible for their behaviors had free will in engaging in those behaviors. That is, they were not coerced, under some type of duress nor mentally impaired (Greene & Cohen, 2004). For these extenuating factors we are likely to forgive, or at least mitigate, the responsibility of the actor if their choices and behaviors end up reflecting negative consequences. But, what does it mean to have free will?

In a poignant discussion of the expectations and bases of our legal system, Greene & Cohen (2004) explain that, in a retributive system such as ours, the criminal responsibility of offenders is based on the notion that free will is incompatible with determinism. Meaning that if certain factors in the life histories, environments or experiences of criminals are motivating factors in their commission of crimes, the legal system is set up so that those factors can be categorically dismissed in favor of privileging the existence of free and rational will. The notion of the role of criminal responsibility and free will shall be discussed in more depth later in this section. First, however, we will look to the empirical data as a way to identify precisely where and in what ways responsibility factors into the meta-narrative of the state and the inmates' vocabularies.

Lesson 14 in the 'Pathway to Change' manual is titled "Becoming More Responsible." The class is asked to come up with every possible excuse they can think of for several hypothetical "real world" problems such as burning dinner, being late, bouncing a check, getting fired or not passing an inspection. The inmates should then decide into which category their excuses fall: "someone else, nobody, me." Once they have decided where their excuses fall, the class is asked to pick the person who made up the "most outrageous" excuse and that person wins a certificate titled 'Most Outrageous Excuse Contest Winner.' The definition of responsibility given to the instructor is: "following through with what you say you'll do." The manual also informs the teacher that an inmate is only taking responsibility when he comes up with excuses that adequately fall into the "me" category.

In the inmates' narratives, this theme of responsibility resonates. The following quotes illustrate how the idea of taking responsibility for past actions and becoming more responsible in the future infiltrates their stories.

ROBERT: When you take drugs, you're not you anymore. What really did make me want to change was how much time I realized I had wasted.

PAUL: It's all on you as an individual.

RONALD: I'm gonna try to do everything different. She [my wife] can't keep me out, only I can keep myself out.

CHAD: You learn: once you keep your hands clean – you gotta stay out of trouble. Everything comes with a price.

AARON: My partying days are done with, now I got responsibilities out there.

DEREK: The only thing that's gonna stop me from breaking the law is when I'm done doing it.

DARIN: My one mistake has kept me down for so long; my own mistakes got me here.

Unlike some other statements made in the narratives, passages reflecting responsibility were frequently characterized with the words "I" and "me." The data indicate that the inmates are aware that taking responsibility is something important to their success outside of prison. Likewise, the Department of Corrections acknowledges that inmates taking responsibility for themselves, their crimes and their behaviors is a key feature in its push toward the cognitive self-change agenda. The Department of Corrections' mission statement indicates that: "we hold offenders accountable for their behavior."

The Missouri Reentry Process likewise acknowledges responsibility as a necessary component to the inmates' successful re-integration into society:

> This partnership will hold offenders responsible for their behavior and accountable for their actions from the day they enter prison through release and community supervision … there are sanctions for those who fail to follow their plans.

Responsibility, then, is characterized as the primary obligation of the offender, while the Department of Corrections exists as the party enforcing accountability. There is little discussion, however, either in the 'Pathway to Change' manual or in Department of Corrections statements of a *shared* responsibility. Being responsible is a concept characterized in these documents as an individual obligation. Nowhere in the 'Pathway to Change' manual do the lessons represent situations occurring in the real world where joint responsibility for events is an acceptable possibility. While the manual acknowledges that the excuses the inmates might make for "unpleasant events" could fall into three categories, "someone else," "nobody" or "me," it indicates that the only "correct" answers are excuses that fall into the "me" category. The mutual exclusivity of the categories provided necessarily funnels all the inmates' experiences into a single static meta-narrative.

Certainly, events occur in everyday social life that may fall into the other two categories or that may not fall into any of the provided categories. There is no alternative provided for the inmates to choose from that would allow them to come up with an excuse for an event where responsibility may be dispersed among several different actors or circumstances. The absence of an "us" category from the existing three indicates that the theme of responsibility as illustrated in the 'Pathway to Change' manual reinforces an either-or dichotomy in the sense that the offending action is either the offender's responsibility, or it is not. Were the inmates provided with an alternative category, the idea that they share partial responsibility for the things that happen in their lives could open up a much more flexible and accessible way of characterizing responsibility in general. Currently, the inmates must take full responsibility for everything that happened to them in their lives as a condition of their release from prison. Adding another possible category in which taking responsibility for one's actions is not so absolute would help to balance the cognitive exercise of helping one's self. It is not my contention that a "shared responsibility" category should replace personal responsibility, rather, I argue that adding another alternative to sole personal responsibility can help keep the storied lives of the inmates from being funneled to extremes. Note that the proposed category is not one of "blame" but one of "sharing." The inmates are faced with a difficult task in trying to talk about the events in their lives while simultaneously taking total responsibility for all of it.

One of the ways in which the inmates seem to work to negotiate the disjuncture between the discourse of the cognitive self-change agenda and their own experiences is by introducing the concept of "blame" into their narratives as an alternative to "taking responsibility." Here, we see how inmates "taking the blame," acts as a buffer between having to take full responsibility for everything that leads them to prison and the knowledge that some of what happened could be attributed to other people. Rather than claim responsibility outright, the inmates manage to acknowledge that they *could* blame others for helping contribute to their actions but, instead, make a point to express their own culpability:

DARRELL: I don't blame no one but myself. I knew the consequences when I put that weed in the trunk.
JOHN: I got myself here – it's up to me to stay out; I don't blame the judge or the cops.
BRIAN: [I blame] myself – because I know I have a lot of sense; what to do and what not to do. I blame myself for being in this situation.
STEVEN: Probably just my time to come. Can't blame nobody but myself.

Further evidence of their management of the role of others is present when they draw on other characters to help build their stories. In their narratives, other players emerge to buttress the actions, motivations, experiences and choices available to the authors. For example:

DAVID: At fourteen years old David's grandfather gave him a pistol and said: "you'll never be broke if you have this."
ROBERT: The foolish girl I was with went into the mall – that's why I'm here.
DARIN: People started opening their mouths, trying to pass the buck to us.
PAUL: Everyone had to be in a gang … [my cousin] collapsed in my arms and died.
JAMES: Ultimately, it was me and the choice I made, but as far as this case goes, it was my ex's family.
RONALD: The cops planted some dope on me.
ALEX: I blame my homeboy. I shoulda not helped this guy but you know, you kind of give up.
ED: I got mixed up with some female, but it was my own fault.
MARTIN: The first time was my fault, it was stupid. This time, I'm gonna have to pin it on my mom.

Certainly, taking responsibility for one's actions seems a noble track. However, when circumstance, the influence of others, unavoidable life events and overbearing hardships are entirely overlooked, the model of responsibility emphasized by the cognitive self-change program is far more repressive than it is liberating. In the same way that the rest of us did not make it to where we are today without the help of others, neither did these inmates make it to prison entirely on their own. Acknowledging that their experiences are deep and dynamic does not necessarily preclude the inmates taking responsibility for their part; it does, however, allow for the black and white of the cognitive self-change agenda to yield to the nuanced relationships and realities experienced in everyday life. The gray area produced as a result is quite present in the inmates' stories and would likely become a useful site of reflection if they were allowed to go there.

Presently, the inmates' narratives are contradictory and fragmented on the issue of responsibility. On one hand, they take on the cognitive self-change agenda in their acknowledgment that they should be solely responsible for their entrance to prison; however, in the same breath they are also relaying stories that implicate other people and circumstances in their path to prison. There is a difference between taking responsibility for one's actions, which the inmates seem to do, and taking sole responsibility for one's entrance into prison, something the inmates are reluctant to claim. Evidence of their reluctance is expressed in their discussions of the negative influence others have had in their lives. The path to prison is characterized as a long and complicated one, according to the stories they tell. Rarely did a single event (or a solitary bad choice) result in their going to prison. The Department of Corrections seems to recognize this fact in its insistence that other people can strongly influence the attitude and actions of the offenders.

In an informational guide published by the Department of Corrections for family and friends of incarcerated individuals, the ideas of emotional support and understanding are emphasized:

> We also encourage you to maintain regular contact with the offender through visits, telephone calls and letters so that you may remain informed of the offender's progress, maintain family ties and provide emotional support (Missouri Department of Corrections, 2009a, 2).

> Many emotions may be felt at this time so it is important that you maintain communication and provide support. It is common for new arrivals to avoid initial contact with family members and friends; this may be due to a variety of reasons. Despite this, please continue to write and be sure to include your full address on the envelope. The offender needs to know you still care and are there for them (3).

> Continued contact with family during and following incarceration can reduce recidivism (Missouri Department of Corrections, 2005, 2).

It is quite clear from these statements that the Department of Corrections acknowledges the strong, positive influence of friends and family on offenders. Simultaneously, however, in its choice to implement the 'Pathway to Change' program, it categorically dismisses the strength of the impact that others can have when the offender engages in *illegal* activity. Failing to acknowledge the influences of others as constant across situations (both positively and negatively) leaves the Department of Corrections in contradiction.

Time after time, according to the inmates' narratives, the most important people in their lives are also culpable parties in their entrance into prison. Allowing the inmates to acknowledge their friends and family as dynamic, imperfect characters in their stories as well as supportive and helpful loved ones would not detract from the message of responsibility, in fact, it may add the validity the inmates seek.

Interestingly, the Department of Corrections and the inmates' narratives ultimately agree that the diffusion of responsibility is a practice that requires the integration of efforts: "the Missouri Reentry Process is a responsibility, which is shared by the offenders, their families, community agencies and the state" (Missouri Department of Corrections, 2006). Choosing to institute an in-prison program that acknowledges the Department of Corrections' own position on allowing joint or diffuse responsibility across a variety of social situations would allow it to maintain its position on accountability and personal responsibility while encouraging relationships with supportive individuals, institutions and agencies. It is contradictory for the Department of Corrections to share responsibility for its own projects and deny that same practice to the inmates. The problem of contradiction here is not simply semantic; the message is a deep one, embedded in this inescapable meta-narrative of the state, the Department of Corrections, the prison and the inmates' own stories (Bosworth, 2007). Discursive inconsistencies like taking sole responsibility for behaviors that were also influenced by situational factors are, much like the idea of always having a choice, not unique to this particular institution.

The responsibility problem

In 1915, Philip Coombs Knapp provided a provocative discussion of criminal responsibility. He stated that most criminals are mentally incapacitated to the point that they commit crimes because they do not know any better. The criminological and greater sociological communities would now see most of the claims he made as grossly overgeneralized but, of course, Knapp was limited by the time period and the availability of extant data on the subject. However, for Knapp, the issue of holding criminals responsible for their behavior was a fundamental flaw in the legal system, not a result of the criminals themselves doing bad things because they were bad people. His argument was that in engaging in retributive justice as a sweeping standardized practice for all criminals, the system neglects the unique and nuanced shades of circumstance and potential for change that surround every individual confronted by the system. For Knapp (1915, 582):

> The punishment ... should fit not the crime but the criminal, just as the object of medical treatment is not the disease but the patient.

The inmates in this study were not found to have been mentally incapacitated, under duress or otherwise incapable of exercising their free will in the commission of their crime, at least based upon the standards of our current tests of legal responsibility. They were, in fact, all found to be responsible for the crime for which they were punished and, in our current system, that also means they were found to have violated the law of their own free will.

Greene and Cohen (2004), however, argue (not dissimilarly from Knapp) that the problem in making assumptions about free will and criminal responsibility is in the tests, procedures and basic premises upon which our current legal system is based. The system itself is flawed in that it ignores strong mitigating factors like environment, circumstance, the influences of childhood and personal relationships. It always favors the notion that if an individual is not mentally handicapped, then he can freely and rationally understand the difference between right and wrong. Upon this premise, then, the system also assumes that if he can understand the difference between right and wrong and chooses to do wrong anyway, then he should be held solely responsible and properly punished.

In working to understand why someone would willfully and rationally commit a crime they know is wrong, they are aware might bring them punishment and for which they will be held responsible, we are forced to look at the general cultural apparatuses that support this analysis of someone's seemingly contradictory behavior. For Greene and Cohen (2004, 1778–9), the problem articulates itself when we ask of the criminal's actions:

> Was it *him*, or was it his *circumstances*? Was it *him*, or was it his *brain*? But what most people do not understand, despite the fact that naturalistic philosophers and scientists have been saying it for centuries, is that there is no "him" independent of these other things.

So, when we take upbringing, genetics, circumstance, neurology and a whole matrix of other extenuating factors into consideration, we can plainly see that free will, in the traditional sense, is not a pure independent condition. Free will is affected by the presence of available alternatives and by the onslaught of unpredictable, often unalterable factors that form the conditions under which a person acts.

Goodenough (2004) expanded this conception of responsibility and free will by calling into question the very act of separating 'criminals' from 'non-criminals.' He provided a good argument against rational choice by asking us to examine our own actions to determine a time when we acted in ways inconsistent with what we knew was "right." Indeed, "loss of control is not something that happens only to some distinguishable other," but something that has happened to all of us, at one time or another. Most of us, however, may be fortunate enough that our circumstances, influential others and personal histories are enough in line with cultural standards of "good" living that we can be excused from, or are at least able to get out of, taking responsibility for much of what we do (Goodenough, 2004, 1806).

As I have demonstrated with the empirical data presented here, taking responsibility for one's actions is a key feature of cognitive self-change practices and the inmates in this study all find a way to do it. Their admissions of responsibility, however, are not without qualification, but it is precisely those qualifying factors that should be taken into consideration. Forcing inmates to say they are solely responsible for their crime is counterproductive. When the environmental, social and cultural circumstances surrounding their lives outside of prison limit their ability to act freely and to rationally choose between right and wrong, further denying them the ability to consider those circumstances as valid simply entrenches them further into a system of flawed moral logic.

Theme three: context

In the same way that choice and responsibility are linked, so too are the contextual elements present in the making of those choices and the difficulty in taking responsibility for them. In fact, it is those very contexts that call into question whether there really is always a choice and how truly responsible the inmates are for their behaviors (Marbley & Ferguson, 2005). This inattention to context is, perhaps, the most egregious flaw in the cognitive self-change model. What happens is that the use of expert knowledge conditions inmates to deny the circumstantial, environmental and interpersonal elements that influence their lives and results in their forced adoption of universal replacement narratives. These replacement narratives are superimposed onto the inmates' personal stories and beliefs through discursive reconstruction. This reconstruction, then, is in turn a more sophisticated form of discipline, enhancing a sense of mental confinement.

The third theme present across all the data sets was that of context. Despite its enduring presence in both the meta-narrative of the state and the personal narratives of the inmates, the theme of context represents a place where the inmates' stories and the institutional data diverge. I define *context* as the ways in which the Department of Corrections and the inmates conceptualize and discuss environment, social realities and life experiences. Then inmates verbalize contexts in the following ways.

DAVID: In my neighborhood, people don't have jobs. They're dealers, prostitutes, users, killers, robbers, home-invaders.

ROBERT: If I didn't change, I knew I'd go back to the same environment I came from.

SAM: Seeing everybody I grew up with was doing wrong. I don't know nothing different – as you can see, all my family here [in prison].

SAM: The police shot my cousin dead in my mom's front yard.

PAUL: Everyone had to be in a gang. [My cousin] collapsed in my arms and died.

PAUL: I wasn't learning any responsibility because she never put her foot down.

GEORGE: I knew it was bound to happen sooner or later. I knew the consequences, I saw my uncles go to prison.

DARRELL: [My old school] was ninety percent whites, ten percent blacks. The place I transferred to was the exact opposite. It wasn't anything I was used to.

RONALD: There were killings, prostitutes, drugs, carjackings, abuse – I come from one of the hardest cities in the world.

CHAD: I put myself in a certain environment. I didn't have to stay on that side of town. I was addicted to it, but it's a cat and mouse game. I know I contradict myself.

DEREK: That's just what everybody did in that area – stole cars; it was a rush.

JAMES: I don't have a drug problem, I have a money problem.

RONALD: That's the hand I was dealt. I'm thirty-one years old and I can recall some things in my head that still make me teary.

The inmates' descriptions of the environments they came from represent a contextual reality that, undoubtedly, played a key role in the events in their lives. The people they know, their addictions, the neighborhoods where they grew up, the deaths of loved ones and feelings of anger for mistreatment by trusted family members are the examples the inmates gave when describing the contexts surrounding their pasts (and presents).

The narratives also indicate that twenty-six of the thirty inmates have had a family member convicted of a crime. From the twenty-six individuals, thirteen were first timers and thirteen were recidivists. This fact, coupled with their stories, illustrates the multi-layered realities these individuals experienced. Their experiences are anything but flat and static; they are thick and contoured descriptions of a lifetime of interactions that have influenced their paths.

The differences between the 'Pathway to Change' class and the narratives are prominent along this theme. Context in the 'Pathway to Change' manual is brought up in Lesson 3: "Environmental Power." The objective of the lesson is "to allow participants to see the affect [sic] that their environment has on their decisions and to help them realize that they can overcome the influence of their environment." One of the activities in the lesson requires the teacher to write the words: fate, nature, and nurture on the chalkboard. The inmates are then given definitions for each concept and told that fate is unchangeable but that nature and nurture are both elements of life that the inmates are able to change. The inmates are then asked to identify certain characteristics as the result of fate, nature or nurture and answer a series of questions to determine what they have learned from the lesson.

The content in the 'Pathway to Change' manual specifically diverges from the inmates' narratives in the way that the ideas of fate, nature and nurture are addressed. For the inmates, "nurture" played an extraordinarily strong role in their life stories. As noted earlier, they rarely *blamed* their environments for their crimes, but they always referenced the contexts surrounding the events in their lives. Statements that indicate "having" to act a certain way given the context of their neighborhoods or the expectations of family members illustrate how embedded their choices and decisions are in the realities of their environment. This theme of addressing context is not dealt with in the same way in the 'Pathway to Change' class. In the class, the inmates are told that they can change both "nature" and "nurture." The only thing they cannot change is "fate." The definition given for nurture includes all the factors the inmates experienced when they were growing up. If it is the case, then, that individuals can really change the factors they experienced growing up, then the manual fails to address precisely how they are supposed to go about making these changes. The manual does not instruct the inmates on how to change (or even overcome) the fact that their mother was a prostitute, their father was a crack dealer and their grandpa gave them a gun at thirteen years old. There is no lesson that teaches them how to change the fact that for a staggering majority, the most important characters in their life stories have also been to prison. Certainly, as evidenced in the Department of Corrections and Missouri Reentry Process statements, "breaking the cycle" of crime is an essential component in reducing recidivism, but there is no indication of how, precisely, the inmates are to do it (Missouri Department of Corrections, 2005; Missouri Department of Corrections, 2006).

Another piece to the theme of context is the fact that most of the men currently in prison are set to return home to the same environments, even the same neighborhoods, they came from. The Missouri Department of Corrections (2005) acknowledges this:

> Over 97% of the people in prison today will someday be released. The vast majority of offenders return to the counties where they lived prior to incarceration.

Its negligence in implementing an in-prison program that acknowledges environmental diversity stands in contradiction with its stated goals. The Department of Corrections instituted the 'Pathway to Change' class in an effort to help reduce the rate of recidivism in Missouri. The 'Pathway to Change' manual's stance that the conditions of one's environment growing up are something that one can retroactively change does not seem to adequately represent the purpose of the Department of Corrections' reentry plan. An acknowledgment of the specific difficulties the inmate has and will face upon release as a direct result of his environment *in addition* to functional suggestions for how he can better handle these conditions would put the Department of Corrections back in line with some of its own claims. The 'Pathway to Change' manual grossly misrepresents the true-to-life contexts faced by the inmates. On this front, the 'Pathway to Change' manual, and by proxy the Department of Corrections, are wholly inadequate in representing the needs, experiences and histories of the inmates.

The context problem

The denial of the conditions surrounding any individual's actions requires viewing reality in a social and cultural vacuum. This denial of context involves separating agency from structure and, thus, individual decision making from the cultural apparatuses that influence those decisions. For Giddens' structuration theory (1984), this separation is impossible. The rules and regulations (structure) of our social world are responsible for both enabling action in some people and constraining it for others. The focus of this theory is on illustrating the inherent differences in the strong relationship between structure and agency in explaining people's potential for action.

For Jeffrey Reiman (2009) the question of context in criminal activity is one that harkens back to responsibility. For Reiman, the way we have set up our institutions of social and criminal justice relies on handing out punishments to wrongdoers without considering the larger social conditions that constrain some and enable others. Using the philosophical principles of Hobbes and Locke to argue that the immorality of criminal action is diminished when the failure of society to protect them is considered, Reiman stated:

> I have less of a moral obligation to respect property in a society that excludes me from the possibility of gaining my own property … many of the people who find themselves convicted of crimes are victims of social injustice. They get less than their rightful share of social benefits. And since the obligation to obey the law is a function of the benefits one receives, it follows that many disadvantaged criminals are not violating their moral obligations to obey the law … because injustice has reduced their obligation to obey the law (125).

For Reiman, the fact that so many of the criminals incarcerated in our prisons today are ensconced in poverty and violent social environments, and experience few opportunities to obtain what we typically consider legitimate success, means that they are, in fact, owed such opportunities by the rest of us. So, he argues that when we deny certain groups of people the same opportunities as everyone else based on social inequalities, their inherent *disadvantage* means that they are less culpable for the crimes they commit because they are less morally bound to respect structural apparatuses such as the law than those who do not experience the same structural inequalities. Criminals, then, are simply taking back what is owed to them by society via the only means available to them. For Reiman, disadvantaged individuals who commit crimes have been historically, culturally and socially denied access to the same opportunities for legitimate success that others have been granted, simply because of *who* they are and *where* they come from. Their moral obligation to follow the law, then, is diminished because, for them, the law does not stand for the same things that it does for others. The law, as structure, simultaneously constrains the agency of the disadvantaged and enables the agency of the advantaged. For Reiman, the diminished obligation to follow the law is a question of morality; this means that disadvantaged people are no less legally obligated to obey the law, but that they cannot be expected to respect part of the social structure that does not benefit them in the same ways that it benefits others.

In applying Reiman's argument to the men in this study, we are forced to consider the contexts surrounding the immediate circumstances leading up to the event for which they were incarcerated, as well as the whole history of familial, personal, social, cultural, environmental, spiritual and physical experiences that paved the way for their entrance into prison. None of the men in this study were currently in prison for committing what we would consider white-collar crimes. The majority of them were in for violating the conditions of their parole or probation for a past crime, many were in for drug possession and several were in for theft, robbery and assault. So, when we pull from their narratives the stories they told of the conditions surrounding their most recent arrest, as well as the stories they told about their neighborhoods, parents, friends and addictions, we see that all of the men in this study were in some way disadvantaged. That is, the overall historical social conditions of their lives made obtaining success in legitimate ways more difficult than for people who do not experience overwhelming inequalities like extreme poverty, abuse or drug addiction.

Understanding the contexts of individual lives allows us to understand why inmates might have committed crimes. Because they cannot expect social structures like the law, education, political opportunity or a capitalist economy to ever benefit them in the same ways they benefit others, the inmates' obligation to respect these structures is reduced. Therefore, their breaking of the law is not as egregious as an advantaged person's breaking of the law because they are simply less morally obligated to follow rules that do not benefit them. Reiman's argument is compelling and (he admits) a radical view of the responsibility of a society to its members. At the very least, it compels us to reconsider the contextual elements of individual lives, the unique ways in which structure constrains the agency of some while enabling it for others, and begs us to think about our collective responsibility for others. For this study, Reiman's argument makes a compelling case for the reintroduction of context back into the discourse of the prison as a way to legitimize the lived experiences of the inmates who find themselves there. This, I argue, is an absolutely essential element in bringing criminal justice into the same arena as social justice.

Theme four: goals

A fourth theme emerged from the narratives and Department of Corrections documents during the process of analysis, further illuminating some commonalities between the inmates' narratives and the institutional narrative. What became important as the interviews progressed was the inmates' acknowledgment of what they hoped to accomplish both in and out of prison. Many of them claimed that they saw prison as both a punishment for their wrongdoings and an opportunity to improve their lives. It was heartening to hear their optimism in the face of unimaginable hardships and the reality of their current incarcerations. The notions of "pulling oneself up by the bootstraps" and "making the best of a bad situation" were thematic elements in the inmates' discussion of the goals they'd set for themselves. Many chose to see their current situations as the springboard for a better life and seemed resolute, even if somewhat confounded, in the thought that they wanted to "do better." The stated goals, as expressed in the interview setting by the inmates, match well with the stated goals of the Department of Corrections and the Missouri Reentry Process. The milestones the inmates claimed to want to achieve for themselves strongly reflected the goals the Department of Corrections claims it wants to achieve to aid offenders. First, we'll look at the specific goals the state and institution expect the inmates to achieve. Then, we will examine the personal goals expressed by the inmates during their interviews. Finally, the juxtaposition of the institutional goals and the inmates' personal goals will be discussed in relation to their relevance, achievability and connection to the cultural meta-narrative compelling similar storylines in our everyday lives.

The institutional goals are stated in the following ways from documents published by the Department of Corrections:

> Offenders can change and be productive citizens … offenders should receive training, education and treatment to better prepare them for transition to the community … offenders should leave the institution as healthy as possible and have access to healthcare in the community … offenders who are better prepared to fulfill their obligations to their children can reduce the intergenerational cycle of crime (Missouri Department of Corrections, 2006).

> The ultimate goal is to produce an "employable offender" (Missouri Department of Corrections 2009b).

These broad-based statements represent the position of the state on its role in the inmates' lives. Breaking intergenerational crime cycles, producing employable offenders and reducing recidivism are what become important for the state, the agents of the state and the institution. These statements are worded in ways that reinforce the state's role as producer. They represent the interests of the state and the taxpaying public, and, seemingly, the inmates. We have come to believe that the government is a service provider for the citizenry, but statements such as these call into question precisely who is considered the consumer and, thus, the party receiving the service. In line with the capitalist goals of a service economy, the Department of Corrections acts as a corporation in order to achieve the ultimate goal of any company, making money. In order to receive financial aid to run its prisons, create jobs, pay policy makers and incarcerate criminals, the state must orient itself in the corporate realm and adopt a business model with which it can achieve its goals. The consumers here are the taxpaying, voting public, and the wording of policies and programs put out by the state are intended for them. If the goals of the state were actually intended to provide services for the *inmates*, they might read a little more closely in line with what the inmates themselves want and need.

The inmates' goals are both different from and similar to the goals the state has lined out as important foci. Here, we see the comparison most prominently when the inmates iterated what they would need to successfully avoid coming back to prison:

JOHN: Staying away from all the bullshit.
DAVID: Lose my 'I don't give a fuck' attitude.

GEORGE: I'll try to live a normal life and see if I like it. I'm tired of that lifestyle.

DARRELL: I'm gonna quit smoking weed.

TIM: I've been trying to teach myself to speak up. I used to look at everything in a negative way, now I'd like to think I'm a more positive person.

JAMES: I don't want this to be the fate of my life. I'm gonna try my hardest, but if things don't go my way, you never know.

RONALD: I'm gonna try and do everything different.

ANDREW: Follow all the bureaucratic bullcrap.

ED: I'm gonna do my best to stay out.

ED: on his plans to enlist in the Armed Forces: "If I did something like that, I'd get the discipline I didn't get growing up."

JAY: Stay busy, work, think of my little girl, go to court, go to church.

BRIAN: Start working, stop hanging around the wrong crowd and think of the people who love [me].

AARON: Sign up for school but don't rush into it ... set long-term goals. It's going to be hard but if it ain't rough, it ain't right.

STEVEN: The first thing I gotta do is work on my thoughts. I have to sit down and actually think about the consequences.

The similarities between the Department of Corrections' goals and the inmates' both involve directing their goals "positively." The Department of Corrections included goals that involve becoming "productive citizens" and the inmates express this sentiment in their desire to get jobs, go to church, go to school and stay out of "trouble," all basic tenets of the meta-narrative of normalcy valued in mainstream American culture. The theme of personal responsibility is also reflected in the inmates' statements about goals. The Department of Corrections stated that inmates "can change," and, indeed, the narratives indicate that the inmates believe that changing from someone who goes to prison to someone who doesn't come back, is an acceptable goal to have. Whether or not they believe they can be successful in achieving that goal is a theme addressed later in this analysis. The similarities between the goals of the state and those of the inmates, however, end there.

The Department of Corrections does not set individually attainable goals; rather, its goals are reflective of ambiguous, longer-term, broader range challenges. Becoming "productive citizens" and "reducing the intergenerational cycle of crime" are fairly large tasks. The goals the Department of Corrections prescribes for the inmates are broad and vague and consist of rather indefinable, intangible markers of success. The inmates' goals, on the other hand, indicate much more immediacy and urgency over a shorter period of time. Staying out of prison and staying away from drugs are the inmates' two most frequently cited goals. These ambitions are highly tangible and quite specific, likely occurring with much struggle. Their completion of these goals is both an immediate and on-going battle beginning before they even leave prison until they fail, or until they don't. While the Missouri Reentry Process involves more than simply inmates' participation in 'Pathway to Change,' such as mandatory drug and alcohol rehabilitation courses, the 'Pathway to Change' class is a missed opportunity to address these issues in relation to the cognitive-skills building and behavioral management principles it espouses.

The Department of Corrections is out of touch with what the inmates believe are their most pressing issues. Certainly, staying out of prison and getting off drugs are the initial steps in becoming a productive citizen and breaking the cycle of crime, but they are also, perhaps, the most difficult. The inmates' self-described goals are the crucial first part of achieving anything else in life, let alone the needs and wants of the state or those expected by the public.

The 'Pathway to Change' manual also directs the inmates' thinking patterns toward the setting of goals. After each lesson, the inmates are instructed to develop 'Mile Markers,' describing what they learned from each lesson and how they can use it to help themselves. Unfortunately, the 'Pathway to Change' manual is, once again, quite vague in its description of how 'Mile Markers' are supposed to help the inmates employ real, tangible solutions to problems they will face upon release. Each lesson has an objective that the inmates are simply asked to "work on" using those objectives to set goals. Without providing a qualitative measure of the appropriateness, relevance or validity of the 'Mile Markers,' the 'Pathway to Change' manual serves simply to instruct, not to guide.

Finally, the Department of Corrections acknowledges the need to work with community organizations, friends and family, church groups and the state to help inmates become "productive citizens" and to help them achieve their goals for successful reintegration back into the community. The breakdown here occurs in the large fissure that exists between the inmates and community resources. Many of the inmates don't know what types of opportunities or resources are available to them upon release or how to access them. The Department of Corrections, via 'Pathway to Change,' is negligent in instructing the inmates on how to achieve its goals for them and especially in how to achieve the goals they have for themselves. In comparison, a college professor cannot expect her students to do well in class if she does not make clear her expectations, how students will be assessed, and where they can learn the material over which they will be tested. In effect, the state sets the inmates up for failure when it encourages them to set lofty goals but neglects to show them precisely how to achieve them.

The goals problem

The problem inherent in the disjuncture between the state's goals for the inmates and the inmates' goals for themselves comes to a head when we consider how this goal-setting is related to the larger issue of prisoner reentry. Reentry, the process of integrating formerly incarcerated inmates back into the free community to live and work, has been sociologists' focus of attention for years. According to the corrections community at large, via practitioners, state and federal policies, programs and politicians, the process of successful community reentry for inmates is essential to their continued success on the outside and the reduction of recidivism. These reentry efforts, however, are often marked in the same ways we have seen through these data: the goals of the state are ambiguous and broad while the goals of the inmates are immediate and specific. As a result, the state neglects to consider many of the specific environmental and social forces that will make transition difficult, but that the inmates know will hinder their successful reintegration.

In their comprehensive article on prisoner reentry, Visher and Travis (2003) identified four interrelated dimensions involved in the transition of inmates from prison back into the community: individual characteristics, family relationships, community contexts and state policies. In their discussion, the authors emphasized the dynamic nature of these elements and how nothing can really be known about successful reentry without examining how these dimensions influence individuals over long periods of time.

In this study, each of these dimensions can be found in the inmates' personal stories and statements about their goals upon release. In the act of taking responsibility for their actions, all of the inmates I interviewed also negotiated their own role in their current incarceration. The 'Pathway to Change' program emphasizes their individual characteristics as the reason for their arrests by telling the inmates that they suffer from flawed thinking patterns. The inmates acknowledge their own shortcomings and many of them expressed the desire to change themselves as part of their goals upon release.

Further, the dimension of family relationships is also evident in the inmates' stated goals. Being better fathers, husbands, sons and brothers and improving their marriages and relationships with other family members became prominent themes in many of the goals they'd set for themselves. In their stories, we saw the difficulty in maintaining relationships with family members who were, themselves, criminals but with whom the inmates maintained very strong bonds. The issue of negotiating family relationships was both a problem and a place for improvement. The role of family in their projections for post-release goals was quite strong, if not somewhat confounding for the inmates who were pulled between their loved ones and the potential negative influence they might have.

Community context as a dimension of reentry, for Visher and Travis (2003) includes "neighborhood-level indicators, such as socioeconomic status, racial diversity and residential stability …" (102). Additionally, the structural makeup of a neighborhood community has a great impact on other elements affecting inmates' potential success, such as the presence of drugs and alcohol, affordable housing, health care and work. The impact of these elements on an inmate's successful reentry, according to Visher and Travis, is important especially when combined with individual factors and family relationships. Community context, then, is perhaps the most unpredictable element the inmates have to overcome upon release.

In many of their narratives the inmates in this study spoke of their neighborhoods in vivid detail and all connected the elements of their community environments to aspects of their offending. However, the inmates were most pessimistic when they discussed the community contexts they would return to after release. By this I mean that when they mentioned changing their thinking patterns or being a better father, the inmates generally seemed more positive about their ability to do these things. In discussing their chances of staying out of prison while living in the neighborhoods and communities they'd come from, they were markedly less sure how those contexts would potentially affect their reentry once they returned. The inmates expressed the most doubt and uncertainty when referencing their environments than they did about any other element in the reentry process.

Finally, state policies also influence the potential success or failure of an inmate transitioning back into the community. Particularly, Visher and Travis (2003) found that reforms of policies determining who goes to prison have led to an overall increase in sentencing length, in-prison policies designed to help prisoners with addiction, job training and education while incarcerated have dramatically decreased and policies that deal with inmates after prison, like conditional releases, probation and parole, have become increasingly more stringent and difficult to follow (see also: Iguchi et al., 2002). The inmates in this study were, at the present time, most affected by the in-prison policies of the state but would soon be faced with the very real issues associated with post-release requirements. 'Pathway to Change' is one of the in-prison programs designed to ease prisoner reentry and community transition and to reduce recidivism. In place of increased vocational, educational or life-skills training, the state chose a program that would restructure inmates' flawed cognitions. The use of expert knowledge by state agents as they hand down wide sweeping policies, such as employing a cognitive self-change agenda, is indicative of just how out of touch the state's goals for the inmates are with the inmates' goals for themselves. The inmates are worried about violating their paroles, staying away from drugs and alcohol and learning how to negotiate poverty, joblessness and family pressures in the immediate future. The state is worried about writing policies and instituting programs that maintain its illusion, in the eyes of the taxpaying consumer base, as a public service provider and benevolent corporate sponsor of the most responsibly flawed members of our society (Bosworth, 2007).

So, the vast differences between the goals the state sets for the inmates and the inmates' personal goals represent a discursive disjuncture that has real-world repercussions. Creating and enforcing oppressive post-release conditions coupled with a deficiency in legitimate aid for the inmates to comply with these conditions while simultaneously ignoring their own concerns for the immediate local struggles awaiting them allows the state to further engage in discipline through all stages in the reentry process. When we critically evaluate the huge fissure created by the state between its expectations for the inmates and their narrated realities, Wayne's statement that: "I don't think there's anything I could have done to stay out. The state likes to keep their hands around your shoulders, bobbing in the pool," seems less like the paranoid delusions of a convicted felon, and more like the very real fears of someone whose intimate familiarity with the system has led to a bleak outlook on his own future potential for success.

Theme five: future

Finally, the fifth theme evident across the data sets was reference to the future. The Department of Corrections and 'Pathway to Change' orient much of their agenda toward the future and, in fact, often intentionally dismiss or downplay any reference to inmates' pasts or histories. Evidence of the program's orientation toward the future is outlined below.

In the 'Pathway to Change' manual, most of the lessons used future-oriented language encouraging the inmates to think ahead and create a plan. The manual sets this theme out in the introduction: "Yesterday is over. You must now focus on what you will do tomorrow. You can continue in the same path, or decide to put this place and these circumstances far behind you." The first lesson in the manual instructs the inmates to create a 'Life Map' where they are to draw a map of their future, setting goals along the way, to help them stay focused on the objectives of the class. Additionally, each lesson begins with an objective, indicating an orientation toward the future wherein the inmates will have completed the lesson or the class and, presumably, have something to show for it. In the 'Pathway to Change' manual, instructions for future orientation include setting 'Mile Markers,' or "where you want to go in life." By consistently directing every lesson and activity in the 'Pathway to Change' class toward going "somewhere" in life, the effect is a forward focus that propels the inmate into the future, whatever that may be.

In creating their 'Life Map,' the manual indicates the inmates should start their map in the present and include potential obstacles that would prevent them from getting to their ultimate goal (whatever it may be). The manual suggests indicating problems like a cheating spouse, misbehaving children, having no money, being in poor health, addiction to alcohol or drugs or not being able to find a job, and then instructing the inmates to include these obstacles in their life map. Next, the inmates are to answer the question: "what do you think you have lost because of poor choices in the past?" The inmates are then asked to come up with an exact dollar amount they have lost because of the poor choices they have made in their past.

What is left out of the 'Life Map' lesson, as well as the rest of the class curriculum, is an acknowledgment of inmates' past accomplishments, successes and the completion of milestones. The 'Pathway to Change' program's insistence on orienting everything positive toward the future seemingly precludes positivity from entering into the inmates' descriptions of their past. Of course, past events helped get them to prison; however, neglecting to celebrate past successes such as the birth of a child, marriage, high school graduation or completion of a GED, getting off drugs or alcohol, helping a family member in need, early release from prison and a multitude of other positive life events leaves the manual to imply that *all* the choices they made in the past were bad ones. Further, if the manual means to indicate that all past events were bad ones, then it also unrealistically indicates that all future choices will be good ones. Here, we see a contradiction between the 'Pathway to Change' program's characterization of the future and the inmates'.

As mentioned earlier in my discussion of the "goals" theme, the inmates set milestones for themselves that are directed positively toward the future. However, the setting of goals and the belief in one's ability to successfully achieve them are two different things. Here, we see the program's characterization of positivity in the future begin to fall apart the moment the "real world" becomes relevant. The inmates' narratives indicated that as they set their goals upon release, their hopes about their ability to achieve them were uncertain, at best:

JOHN: I just hope one day soon, I can learn the word 'no.'

GEORGE: I probably will sell [drugs] again, just to get back on my feet. The poor have no choice but to do this.

DARRELL: The worst part of it is going to be the record. I'll be a convicted felon.

TIM: If I come back it will be on a parole violation.

JAMES: Only thing I can see coming back here for is money – selling drugs. I do love [my girlfriend] enough to not come back but who's to say what happens once I get out of here?

DAN: To be honest, I won't know till I get out.

RONALD: [My biggest obstacle] is knowing what the right thing is to do but not doing it.

ALEX: [In response to my question if he believed he would ever be back in prison] Yes, I ain't found myself yet.

REGGIE: I don't have a problem staying out of trouble, I got a problem violating on technicalities. I know I gotta do something different. It's inevitable; I'll come back on violations.

ED: I'm gonna do my best to stay out.

BRIAN: I didn't feel like giving up. I know now, you might as well give up. Depends on when I get out – how I see myself.

AARON: [On if he thought he would go back to prison] I don't really think so. If it happens, then it's meant to happen.

DEREK: I can't even say for sure I'm not coming back. I hope to God I don't come back.

The language used by these men to discuss the future is flooded with uncertainty, insecurity and fear. These statements stand in stark contrast to their acknowledgment of the need to take personal responsibility. If they truly believed (as the Department of Corrections and 'Pathway to Change' would have them think) that all it takes to stay out of prison is to become responsible and make "good choices," then their characterizations of the future would look very different. Their pronounced uncertainty in their ability to stay out of prison once released is indicative of how much weight they give to changing their thinking patterns and simply making good choices as strategies for staying out. If they truly believed, as the program tells them, that all they need to do to have a successful future is to forget their pasts and make better decisions, it would seem that their characterizations of their potential success would be more optimistic. Their inability to do so, then, speaks to their lack of faith in the ideas and strategies set forth in the class.

The meta-narrative, as espoused by the expert knowledge of corrections officials, professors of Theater and Film, prison guards and housing unit staff, insists on the inmates' participation in positively orienting all future dreams and behaviors. While acknowledging that there will be obstacles to success in the future, the experts do little to realistically orient and empirically ground their programs in the needs and struggles of the people they claim to help. The inmates, on the other hand, understand their chances of staying out of prison have more to do with the circumstances and situations they face once they get out than they do with looking on the bright side. An inmate who leaves prison with all the best intentions but without the practical skills, a realistic vision of the struggles he will face and, perhaps, even a helping hand sees his chances of staying out of prison significantly diminish.

The future problem

According to large-scale, meta-analytical studies assessing the efficacy of cognitive-behavioral programs, like the one presented in this book, on reducing rates of reoffending, the consensus is that they work (Lipsey et al., 2001; Landenberger & Lipsey, 2005; Wilson et al., 2005; Wormith et al., 2007). Lipsey et al. (2001) found that in-prison cognitive-behavioral therapy programs using a quasi-experimental or experimental design, given to the general inmate population rather than specialized subsets, and focusing centrally on changing inmates' thinking patterns, are effective among adult and juvenile offender populations at reducing their rates of reoffending over time. Landenberger and Lipsey (2005) confirmed these findings but emphasized that the success of individuals in these programs hinges on the quality of the content in the programs (see also: Andrews & Dowden, 2005). Higher quality programs with few internal inconsistencies were more effective at reducing rates of reoffending.

What is important to note about these studies is that they used data from the state to outline the criteria for the programs they evaluated, as well as individual rates of reoffending. This is problematic because, as we've seen from this study, the state's conception of the programs it enforces in prisons can be very different from the reality of the material and content actually being taught. Further, it is important to note that recidivism and reoffending have sometimes been used interchangeably in subsequent reviews of these meta-analyses when they are, in fact, two very different things.

Recidivism typically refers to an instance where an individual who was previously incarcerated returns to prison. The reasons for the return to prison are variable and broad and can include anything from the commission of a new crime to a technical violation of parole or probation. Reoffending generally refers to an individual who was previously convicted of a crime and punished for it, committing a new, unrelated crime and receiving new punishment as a result of that conviction. The inattention to the meanings of these different terms is problematic because state and federal governments have used academic studies that only look at the positive effects of cognitive-behavioral therapies in prison on rates of *reoffending* to inform policies based on their recommendations to argue for cognitive-behavioral programs' effectiveness against *recidivism* (Milkman & Wanberg, 2007; Clark, 2010). The Missouri Department of Corrections, the National Institute of Justice and the National Institute of Corrections via the U.S. Department of Justice have all referenced academic meta-analyses favoring a reduction in reoffending through cognitive-behavioral therapy programs in prison to argue for their widespread use in prisons as a way to reduce recidivism. The reality is that the government is confounding reoffending rates with recidivism rates when few of the meta-analyses actually even looked at the effects of cognitive-behavioral therapy on overall recidivism. This lack of understanding of the recommendations from academics has led to poor policy decisions by the federal and state governments and the cooptation of good, scientific research as a justification for the continued implementation of bad programs.

Additionally, very few studies have been done that use in-depth qualitative research methods to look at the inner workings of these cognitive-behavioral therapy programs in prison. The result is that much of what is actually happening through discourse in the disciplinary space is being overlooked. And so, again, it is time to ask not "what works," but "at what cost?"

It is no wonder that the inmates in this study felt ambiguous about their futures. For them, staying out of prison is not so much a question of whether or not they will reoffend; many of them believe that they won't. The more pertinent issue for the inmates in this study was whether or not they would come back to prison, that is, recidivate. They were much more reticent to claim that they would never come back. They "hoped," "prayed," and vowed to "try" not to return to prison, but their overall sentiment about their chances of staying out, in the face of extreme parole conditions, neighborhood and family contexts as well as drug addiction and a failing job market, was entirely uncertain.

These five common themes: choice, responsibility, goals, context and future occurred across all the data sets and in every narrative. They are the guiding thread connecting the Department of Corrections, the program and the inmates together, but they are also the heavy burden separating them. The state, as meta-narrative, and the inmates, as lived reality, are intimately connected. In prison, it is bureaucracy and policy that guide every waking moment of an inmate's life, but outside they fend for themselves. Reality is not tied to practicality here and yet, when the inmates eventually fail and return to prison, the state continues to wonder why.

References

Andrews, D. A. & Dowden, C. (2005). Managing correctional treatment for reduced recidivism: A meta-analytic review of programme integrity. *Legal and Criminal Psychology, 10*, 173–87.

Bosworth, M. (2007). Creating responsible prisoners: Federal admission and orientation packs. *Punishment and Society, 9*(67), 67–85.

Clark, P. (2010). Preventing future crime with cognitive behavioral therapy. *National Institute of Justice Journal, 265*, 22–5.

Giddens, A. (1984). *The constitution of society: Outline of the theory of structuration.* Oakland: University of California Press.

Goodenough, O. R. (2004). Responsibility and punishment: Whose mind? A response. *Philosophical Transactions: Biological Sciences, 359*(1451), 1805–9.

Greene, J. & Cohen, J. (2004). For the law, neuroscience changes nothing and everything. *Philosophical Transactions: Biological Sciences, 359*(1451), 1775–85.

Iguchi, M. Y., London, J. A., Forge, N. G., Hickman, L., Fain, T. & Riehman, K. (2002). Elements of well-being affected by criminalizing the drug user. *Public Health Report, 17*(1), 146–50.

King, J. B. (1988). Prisoner's paradoxes. *Journal of Business Ethics, 7*(7), 475–87.

Knapp, P. C. (1915). Criminal responsibility. *Journal of the American Institute of Criminal Law and Criminology, 6* (4), 571–85.

Landenberger, N. A. & Lipsey, M. W. (2005). The positive effects of cognitive-behavioral programs for offenders: A meta-analysis of factors associated with effective treatment. *Journal of Experimental Criminology, 1*(4), 451–76.

Lipsey, M. W., Chapman, G. L. & Landenberger, N. A. (2001). Cognitive-behavioral programs for offenders. *Annals of the American Academy of Political and Social Science, 578*, 144–57.

Marbley, A. F. & Ferguson, R. (2005). Responding to prisoner reentry, recidivism and incarceration of inmates of color: A call to the communities. *Journal of Black Studies, 35*(5), 633–49.

Milkman, H. & Wanberg, K. (2007). Cognitive-behavioral treatment: A review and discussion for correctional professionals. U.S. Department of Justice: National Institute of Corrections.

Missouri Department of Corrections. (2005). *Missouri makes its move.* Available online at http://doc.mo.gov/mrp/mrp.php.

—— (2006). Missouri reentry process principles. Available online at http://doc.mo.gov/mrp/mrp.php.

—— (2009a). Family and friends resources. Available online at http://doc.mo.gov/programs.php.

—— (2009b). Strategic plan. Available online at http://doc.mo.gov/mrp/mrp.php.

Reiman, J. (2009). The moral ambivalence of crime in an unjust society. In J. Reiman and P. Leighton (Eds.), *The rich get richer and the poor get prison: A reader.* New York: Pearson.

Sugden, R. (1991). Rational choice: A survey of contributions from economics and philosophy. *The Economic Journal, 101*(407), 751–85.

Visher, C. A. & Travis, J. (2003). Transitions from prison to community: Understanding individual pathways. *Annual Review of Sociology, 29*, 89–113.

Wilson, D. B., Bouffard, L. A. & Mackenzie, D. L. (2005). A quantitative review of structured, group-oriented, cognitive behavioral programs for offenders. *Criminal Justice and Behavior, 32*(2), 172–204.

Wormith, S. J., Althouse, R., Simpson, M., Reitzel, L. R., Fagan, T. J. & Morgan, R. D. (2007). The rehabilitation and reintegration of offenders: The current landscape and some future directions for correctional psychology. *Criminal Justice and Behavior, 34*(7), 879–92.

9 Demolition

"It's going to be hard but if it ain't rough, it ain't right."

Aaron, 23

The empirical data in this book have, thus far, provided a backdrop for the formulation of a theory of discursive discipline. These data have allowed us to see the inner workings of the systemic oppression of personal narratives and the replacement of them with a single culturally approved master narrative. In prison, even in the absence of any particular cognitive-behavioral program, discursive discipline is the guiding way of life for the inmates there. Their words, responses, ideas and stories are constrained by the social forces of disciplinary control. Inmates in prison are only allowed to speak in certain ways, at certain times and about certain things during the course of their confinement. Failure or refusal to engage in the state-controlled meta-narrative results in their further discipline. This form of discipline is distinctly different from their physical or social confinement; it is enacted discursively, through words, stories, text and policy and is characterized as the 'right way' of thinking. As a result, the disciplinary nature of this sort of discursive control emerges as another way to oppress, control and limit the inmates' actions. Guised in the rhetoric of rehabilitation, reentry and cognitive change, discursive discipline is a highly effective way to create a more controllable population. By telling the inmates that the problem lies within them and by setting itself up, through the use of expert knowledge, as the sole purveyor of what is right and wrong, the state is able to act as a disciplinary puppet master; physically, socially and discursively pulling all the strings.

In the following sections, we'll examine how discursive discipline is precisely enacted through the use of 'expert knowledge' as a source of unquestionable truths, how lived realities are suppressed in favor of the common meta-narrative and, finally, the possibility of where these processes of control can be found in other social arenas. The following discussion requires a shift in perspective from thinking of inmates as prisoners confined in an institution to seeing them, once again, as humans entrenched in the same social processes as the rest of us. Taking this perspective will help illuminate the myriad ways in which each of us may be subjected to discursive discipline and, in fact, may even help to reproduce it in our everyday lives.

Expert knowledge versus lived realities: creating discursive discipline

If we look precisely at where layers of discourse converge, we can see several different levels of narrative working together. Loseke (2007) noted that the various types of identities created through narrative are not separate phenomena, but are layered, embedded stories that influence and affect one another. Here, we see that discursive discipline is enacted at each of these levels of narrative identity: cultural, institutional, organizational and personal.

For Loseke, narrative identity at the cultural level is expressed through master narratives that explicate certain common groupings among individuals and provide classifications that help us to organize our social world. Stories at the cultural level are being constructed constantly and those delivered by "professionals or scientists" are typically received in higher regard by the general public than those stories told by "disadvantaged people," which are typically ignored (665). The cultural stories in this study are the broad-based meta-narratives that delineate "good" law-abiding citizens from "bad" criminals. The persistent themes across these cultural narratives are personal responsibility, personal blame, individuality, hard work, patriotism, doing the right thing and a myriad of other values that Americans tend to believe makes someone a "good" citizen. These cultural stories are told by politicians, lobbyists, policy makers, the media, teachers, scientists and other agents of institutions benefiting from their propagation. In the construction of these broad-based meta-narratives, our social world is classified and separated into binaries which allow us to use "symbolic codes" to more easily make sense of the world (Loseke, 2007).

Cultural stories, then, are necessarily disciplinary in nature. When agents of cultural narratives, such as policy makers or directors of state prisons, are able to benefit from establishing cultural binaries like the establishment of "good" taxpayers versus "bad" offenders, the result is that when they align themselves with the majority they unfailingly win their support. So, it is in the interests of those writing policy and running prisons to appropriate the cultural narrative themes of personal responsibility, punishment for crimes and medicalization and use them in ways that make the general public believe that there really *are* differences between them and the "bad" others (Clawson & Trice, 2000). We, as the everyday law-abiding public are controlled through these discursive binary constructions. We believe in these cultural stories because, we've been told, we are the good ones. We take responsibility for our actions, we pull ourselves up by our proverbial bootstraps, we work hard and help others but don't take handouts ourselves. These general cultural stories allow us to reinforce the vast differences that we want to see between who *we* are, and who *they* are. But, by virtue of the fact that these stories are inherently not our own, we are controlled by the most believable experts and whatever stories they tell us are relevant. We formulate our own histories based on these general cultural narratives and incorporate those collective themes into our retrospective accounts of our own lives. We are discursively disciplined, just like the inmates, if we cannot or will not adopt the language of the cultural narrative.

Through my analyses of the inmates' narratives, statements from the Missouri Department of Corrections and the content in the 'Pathway to Change' manual, it is clear that the cognitive self-change agenda instituted in the prison is designed to rewrite the experiences and stories of the inmates into an approved cultural meta-narrative that emphasizes sole and individual responsibility, blame, personal decision making and the potential to change in a contextual vacuum. By themselves, the concepts of taking responsibility for one's actions and making good life decisions are highly reflective of the American values most of us find important. But, when stripped of the array of experiences within which "good decisions" and "personal responsibility" are necessarily embedded, the result is a minefield of uncertainties (Gubrium & Holstein, 2001).

In prison generally and through these cognitive self-change classes particularly, the expert knowledge of professors, politicians and justice administrators is pitted against the lived realities of the incarcerated inmates. The two sides are locked in battle where the struggle to stay on top is reiterated in a multitude of ways; each side fighting for its own voice to be heard; but the fight isn't fair. The institution gets to decide, by virtue of having a list of "experts" to consult, how the inmates should think of themselves and their pasts, how they are allowed to speak of their lives and what they must repeat in order to earn their freedom.

For the purposes of this study, I have used *expert knowledge* to refer to the tools and resources used by scholars and administrators to inform programs in prison. By virtue of their positions in places of some repute, "experts" are able to use their knowledge to wield power over others. Here, the expert knowledge stems primarily from one source; the creator of the 'Pathway to Change' program implemented by the Department of Corrections in Missouri. As noted earlier, the creator of 'Pathway to Change' is an Associate Professor of Theater and Film and has been a key player in bringing the cognitive self-change agenda to states across the country for a number of years. He has consulted with many corrections and court systems and his work has been used in Texas, North Dakota, Georgia, Missouri, Michigan and Utah. Professor Nelson is also the president of a self-help-like corporation and sells his programs to various Departments of Correction and justice facilities. According to documentation from the Missouri Department of Corrections, Professor Nelson's 'Pathway to Change' class was the most affordable package available employing the cognitive self-change agenda. So, in the adoption of these types of programs, the state, likewise, becomes a disseminator and producer of expert knowledge.

The prison requires inmates' perceived internalization of expert knowledge before they can be released. The restructuring of thinking patterns is not restricted to simply changing one's point of view, but the inmates are also expected to change their own experienced histories. The "restructuring of thinking patterns" then turns into the rewriting of lives. The denial of individuality is the aftermath of the cognitive self-change program. Imposing expert knowledge in this way and the coerced rewriting of individual histories is what I call *discursive discipline*. By suppressing *lived realities*, the experience-based life stories, narratives and histories told by the inmates, the institution is able to control them, en masse, by eliciting guilt and enforcing self-blame. The suppression of individual stories and contexts by the institution onto the inmates is oppressive. It restricts and constrains their possibilities for self-conceptualization, reflexivity and future action. The absolute requirement that the inmates at least regurgitate the principles of cognitive self-change as a condition of their release is disciplinary, not corrective.

The experience of being a member in a cognitive self-change class creates a double-edged sword: if the inmates resist the program's principles they are punished with the possibility of not being released from prison; yet, in their very articulation of those principles, the inmates are likewise punished by being forced to forego what they know to be their own truths and submit to an alternative reality, created through meta-narrative by the prison. This discursive discipline becomes the source of confusion, uncertainty and resignation for the inmates. Yet, from the perspective of the institution, it creates a much more controllable population of offenders. It is as Foucault (1979, 202–3) saw it:

> He who is subjected to a field of visibility, and who knows it, assumes responsibility for the constraints of power; he makes them play spontaneously upon himself; he inscribes in himself the power relation in which he simultaneously plays both roles; he becomes the principle of his own subjection.

In stripping individuality from the stories and experiences of their lives, the institution eliminates resistance in favor of complacency and uniformity.

If this study were designed to determine whether or not the state meta-narrative works to change inmates' cognitions and self-concepts, then I would deem it a success. The goal is to restructure thinking patterns and the cognitive self-change program certainly does that as evidenced through the contradictory and competing languages and stories used by the inmates to articulate their experiences. They used the words they learned in class to try to describe their lives during our interviews. However, in every case those words were inadequate. They needed more than a vocabulary of solitary responsibility to explain who they were and why they were in prison. They struggled with words like "choice" and "blame" in trying to describe their path to prison and they always referenced the influence of other characters. So, the cognitive self-change program effectively infiltrates the language inmates use to tell their stories, but it also oppresses the individuality of experiences that stem from those narratives. The result is a population of inmates, soon to be released, who are forced to claim sole responsibility for being in prison but, when asked, are almost entirely without confidence about their chances of staying out.

The effect of discursive discipline is a tangled and confusing mess of contradictions. The institution contradicts itself by publicly stating goals that differ considerably from its chosen method of implementation in the principles of cognitive self-change. The inmates contradict themselves by telling their truths through stories, all the while working hard to maintain the language of the cognitive self-change program, despite the fact that it constrains what they're allowed to say and think. Most confounding, perhaps, is the inmates' acknowledgment of their own contradictory statements. Many of the interviewees stated that they realized what they were saying "didn't make sense" or wasn't the "right" way of thinking.

The practice of implementing any mandatory program that intentionally attempts to "change" something about a person is an exercise in power and control. Because the concept of change is not value neutral, the result is the insistence that there is only one correct path for every person. Expert knowledge defines normalcy and deviance very specifically. It draws out, in great detail, what a person's life should look like, how their thoughts should sound, what words should come out of their mouths, what futures they ought to dream and what actions they must take. The fabric of the cognitive self-change tapestry is a uniform representation of acceptable reality under which every inmate becomes subsumed. Alternative narratives are dangerous and resistance to the program is characterized as an unwillingness to change (Fox, 1999).

The fact that every inmate must not only take the cognitive self-change class, but also graduate as a condition of their release effectively turns the program from a (perhaps) well-intentioned, if misguided, attempt to reduce recidivism into a highly effective form of discursive discipline. The result is a graduation from Foucault's "docile bodies" to the creation of docile minds. To engage in the production of *docility of the mind*, the "experts" tear down the inmates' individual realities by devaluing their pasts. In forcing the inmates to deny the events, choices, people and circumstances (both good and bad) that they experienced prior to entering prison, experts are able to place themselves in a much more strategic position of power, as if the erasure of pasts creates a clean slate upon which the cognitive self-change agenda can be etched.

Due to the competing nature of expert knowledge and lived realities in prison, my project now becomes about finding a way to bridge the gap between the imposition of the institutional meta-narrative and the personal histories and unique futures of the prison inmates. I believe that these narratives do not necessarily have to contradict one another. I believe that revisions to existing policy can create a program that brings the institution's long-term recidivism-reduction plans and the inmates' short-term survival goals much closer and much more realistically together.

Oppressive methods in the exercise of control

In order to begin the project of reconciling the plans of the institution with the needs of the inmates, the methods through which the institution reaches the inmates must be changed. It is evident that the 'Pathway to Change' cognitive self-change plan as the primary method of connection between the parties is inadequate. The goals of the institution are to help the inmates become "productive" citizens and to help keep them from coming back to prison by obtaining an education, employment and stable living environment; the inmates' goals are essentially the same. The piece that doesn't make sense for achieving these goals is in the total restructuring of the inmates' thinking patterns through the erasure of past experiences and the denial of context. In fact, there is very little about the cognitive self-change program that aligns with the stated goals of the institution at all.

The lessons encouraged in the program are impractical, non-functional, poorly based representations of the inmates' actual experiences. The cognitive self-change program requires the inmates to engage in activities that many grown adults might consider degrading and infantilizing. They are required, in this mandatory prison class, to play games, draw with crayons, dress up in costumes, perform skits and have story time. In Lesson 4, the inmates must determine who has the best values: Lynn the Late, Gari the Gossip, Willie the Witness, Pat the President or Chris the Carefree. Lesson 5 encourages the inmates to better understand the concept of self-esteem by having the instructor play a recording of Whitney Houston singing *The Greatest Love of All*. Lesson 18 requires the inmates to learn keys to better communication by playing the "telephone game," wherein they whisper in one another's ears, following the fictional "Patty" on her alliterative quest to find pumpernickel bread.

Only one lesson, at the end of the program, deals with teaching the inmates how to answer a job ad. Any practical application of the cognitive self-change concepts to situations occurring in the "real world" is lost. In a place inherently charged with hyper-masculinity, racial tensions, violence and an often poorly regulated system of authority, the fact that these men are being treated like children, with no connection to how these exercises will translate or help them once they're released, is dangerous.

The fact that 'Pathway to Change' is based upon concepts derived from programs that teach children cognitive skills, speaks to the bases for its content (Insight Learning Foundation, 2009, George Nelson curriculum vitae). Inmates in prison are not children and their treatment as such is an exercise in negligence. The idea that criminals are sub-human, childlike or ignorant is a characterization that was discarded by the scientific community over a century ago.

In shuffling prison inmates into categories that label them as childlike, flawed, ill or otherwise incapable of helping themselves, the state further establishes the "good/bad" cultural binary that allows it to act as a controller and corrector of these problem individuals. The environment of the prison is highly structured and this structure is what allows expert knowledge to dominate individual lives by limiting their possibilities for alternative action (Paterniti, 2000). Institutional selves, lodged within the organization structure of the prison and the cultural apparatus of our collective social world become what Gubrium and Holstein called "deprivatized" (2001). People's stories are no longer unique to themselves, but have been created for them, in public spaces, through any number of cultural, organizational and institutional media. In the making of institutional identities, through the construction and imposition of acceptable master-narratives onto individual lives, actors are submitted to a comprehensive exercise in control. The controlling nature of prison life is simply a reification of the discursive discipline present in the ways our cultural discourses are constructed for us.

The shaping of narratives that individual actors are then expected to assume as their own has been documented in other social institutions as well. For Goffman (1961), the mental institution was one of the arenas where total confinement went beyond the physical apparatuses of walls and barred windows and entered into the realm of mental confinement. According to Goffman (1961, 151–2):

> In the mental hospital, the setting and the house rules press home to the patient that he is, after all, a mental case who has suffered some kind of social collapse on the outside, having failed in some over-all way, and that here he is of little social weight, being hardly capable of acting like a full-fledged person at all.

The medicalization of criminal behavior (as we've seen from the data in this study) reveal the striking similarities between what Goffman observed for mental patients and the ways in which inmates in prison are discursively disciplined.

Leslie Paik (2006) found similar processes of identity construction in the rewriting of personal experiences through talk in a therapeutic drug treatment facility. Paik discovered that individuals in her sample were often guided by staff and other participants into establishing themselves via a "dope fiend" identity. Used as a frame of reference for who they were and why they were in the program in the first place, the "dope fiend" identity was buttressed by institutional characterizations of what dope fiends were like (unable to control their emotions, misguided, angry, recovering). Clients in the program were encouraged to "act as if" they were recovering, however, the very suggestion to do so from staff immediately called into question the sincerity of the client's subsequent talk and behaviors.

Joseph Hopper (2001) also found institutional constructions of identity occurring in the processes of divorce proceedings. Hopper noted that there are two contradictory conceptions of self at work in divorce cases. The "moral self" is the identity typically taken on by the clients, the people who are getting the divorce. This conception of self allows the clients to construct their position in the divorce proceedings against their partner's and simultaneously allows them to maintain what they consider to be socially acceptable conceptions of people getting divorced. This moral self is inherently at odds with the self that lawyers and other professionals working on divorce cases tend to construct for their clients. Constructing a "legal self" for their clients allows professionals to better negotiate the legal processes of the court system, thus allowing them to do a better job at representing their client and giving them a better shot at winning. Legal professionals tend to encourage their clients to claim ownership of the "legal identity" as a way for them to see their own case for what it is: an amoral and logical legal exchange whereby the established rules are rational and static.

Institutional professionals shape their clients' identities through a process that engages in discursive discipline:

> Attorneys also sometimes strengthen the salience of clients' moral selves by maneuvering them into doing the "right" thing – what is required of the legal self – by drawing upon clients' moralistic interpretations of how a divorce is playing out. "You sometimes have to play into their craziness," one attorney explained (2001, 138).

So, this conception of how to negotiate the landscape of a social institution like divorce court is conceived by the agents of the institution as a meta-narrative of success, discursively overshadowing the lived realities and moral selves of the clients. This "for your own good" justification is something we've likewise seen in the prison system. The cognitive self-change agenda is housed in the rhetoric of rehabilitation and easy transition. An inability or refusal to adopt the institutional self is characterized as the inmates getting in their own way, just as Hopper found that divorcing people were seen as getting in their own way by failing to adopt the legal self that was pushed on them by their attorneys.

Finally, Susan E. Chase (2001) found that students' voices concerning diversity and, in particular, personal sexual identity, were influenced by the policies, programs, practices and discourses of the universities they attend. Chase noted that the discursive culture of a school is able to significantly enable or constrain the personal discourses of individuals. Schools, then, act as the guiding force of social discourse regarding personal conceptions of self and identity. Some schools have more open policies about students' right to express themselves and their identities, other schools are less likely to entertain notions of difference, diversity and the expression of self. In each situation, the individual actors' voices, stories and discourse are shaped by the available freedom within the educational and cultural setting of the school. So, Chase showed that institutional policies shape individuals' realities and conceptions of who they are in very real ways.

In this chapter I have argued that discursive discipline is culturally pervasive in the sense that the values and ideals espoused by individuals in our society are reflective of a master narrative that we adopt for fear of being different or seeming "bad." This fear of entering into the category of the "other" has helped establish the cultural binary that allows us to medicalize criminals' behaviors and enact policies that permit us to fix their flaws. Particularly, discursive discipline can be found at the institutional level in a number of different arenas. We have seen the same processes of institutional identity construction emerge in legal, medical, therapeutic, educational and correctional settings. The construction of the institutional self occurs in everyday life through the institutions we have set up to frame our lives and our identities. Discursive discipline is more than the formulation of institutional or cultural meta-narratives and people's adoption of them; it is the specific ways in which individuals are coerced to rewrite their personal histories in ways that make them more easily controllable. There is no conductor leading our actions or choreographer influencing our behaviors, but there are cultural ways of understanding the self and resistance to those understandings is met with a unique form of discipline.

What is necessary to begin to reconcile the fissure caused as a result of the effects of discursive discipline between the institution and prison inmates is the recognition that the imposition of a single meta-narrative is ineffective. Creating a bridge between the institution and the inmates is what will allow for both the teaching of functional concepts and the practical application of course content to the real world. The first building block in creating this bridge is in redefining what is meant by "expert knowledge."

References

Chase, S. E. (2001). Universities as discursive environments for sexual identity construction. In Gubrium, J. F. & Holstein, J.A. (Eds.), *Institutional selves: Troubled identities in a postmodern world.* (pp. 142–56). New York: Oxford University Press.

Clawson, R. A. & Trice, R. (2000). Poverty as we know it: Media portrayals of the poor. *The Public Opinion Quarterly, 64*(1), 53–64.

Foucault, M. (1979). *Discipline and punish: The birth of the prison.* New York: Second Vintage Books.

Fox, K. (1999). Changing violent minds: Discursive correction and resistance in the cognitive treatment of violent offenders in prison. *Social Problems, 46*(1), 88–103.

Goffman, E. (1961). *Asylums: Essays on the social situation of mental patients and other inmates.* New York: Anchor Books.

Gubrium, J. F. & Holstein, J. A. (2001). *Institutional selves: Troubled identities in a postmodern world.* New York: Oxford University Press.

Hopper, J. (2001). Contested selves in divorce proceedings. In Gubrium, J. F. & Holstein, J.A. (Eds.), *Institutional selves: Troubled identities in a postmodern world* (pp. 127–41). New York: Oxford University Press.

Insight Learning Systems. (2009). *Personnel summary.* Available online at www.insightlearning.com/Home.asp.

Loseke, D. R. (2007). The study of identity as cultural, institutional, organization and personal narratives: Theoretical and empirical integrations. *The Sociological Quarterly, 48*, 661–88.
Paik, L. (2006). Are you truly a recovering dope fiend? Local interpretive practices at a therapeutic community drug treatment program. *Symbolic Interaction, 29*(2), 213.
Paterniti, D. A. (2000). The micropolitics of identity in adverse circumstance: A study of identity making in a total institution. *Journal of Contemporary Ethnography, 29*, 93–119.

10 Rebuilding

"You'll have to have success stories."

Joseph, 42

Reconciling difference through the redefinition of meanings

Discursive discipline is enacted through the social institutions and cultural narratives that influence all of us; but it is highly pervasive in our prison and correctional systems. The practice of enforcing discursive discipline through the forced rewriting of individual histories into a common state-approved meta-narrative has left an immense gap between the methods of recidivism reduction used by the state and the practical, real world concerns expressed by the inmates. Cognitive-behavioral programs have been found to be somewhat effective at reducing rates of reoffending and, in some cases, also rates of recidivism. The quantitative data used to determine these results, however, is lacking in measures that can tell us about the quality of the programs, relevance of the programs to the inmates' needs, internal methodological consistency of the material, long-term social and psychological consequences of inmates' participation or the short-term effects of coerced performance in group settings.

The task now is in designing research projects that can address the issues neglected by large meta-analyses. It seems that state and federal departments of correction and justice are pleased enough with the results of quantitative studies claiming cognitive-behavioral programs reduce rates of reoffending and recidivism, since these studies are so frequently referenced. Our job now becomes finding ways to fill in the gaps in the research while also making our suggestions for program revisions amenable to policy makers. Making practical, translatable, workable policy suggestions to lawmakers and corrections professionals does not mean that we, as social scientists, have to neglect making critical analytical and theoretical interpretations of our data. It simply means that we have the responsibility and the opportunity to act in ways that critique the status quo while also helping to produce real-world change that can bring about social justice for our participants.

In order to begin to build a more functional bridge between the Department of Corrections and the individual inmates, the meanings behind each party's goals and the realities of getting there must be redefined. In aligning the inmates' realities with the resources available to the state and the institution, the result is the mutual construction of a much more sturdy, realistic and practical program where shared meanings, unique experiences and individual efforts are supported, rather than torn down.

In the next sections I outline the ways in which key features of the current system can be redefined to become more inclusive of the players entrenched in the prison setting. I then use these newly redefined concepts to argue for a collaborative model of recidivism reduction, which involves shifting the focus of sole responsibility and blame from the inmates and repositioning it so that the onus of accountability is more equally shared among everyone involved in the processes of justice, including the inmates, the state, policy makers, corrections professionals and the public at large. I conclude with some suggestions for the next steps researchers and practitioners can take to continue the critical evaluation of these programs and my hopes for the future of this field of inquiry and the sociology of prisons in general.

Expert knowledge

Instead of segregating inmates' stories and lived realities from the content of a prison class, the institution can implement a much more functional program by allowing the inmates to embrace their differences while integrating their unique, experience-based stories. Making such a move will require redefining what is considered "expert knowledge." The individuals who have actually lived through difficult life experiences, personal struggles, arrest and imprisonment are the only people who can truly be called "experts" on those matters. The redefinition of what counts as valid and applicable knowledge is necessary to empowering, rather than devaluing, the inmates' lives. The inmates are the experts of their own experiences, and their insights into what they face in the "real world" signal the transformation of lived realities into expert knowledge.

There is a wealth of insight, information, knowledge, wisdom and understanding waiting to be tapped in the stories and narratives the inmates tell. If they are now using Foucault's self-regulation and internalized discipline to make the forces of power "play spontaneously on themselves," then they can just as well use those same energies to enable transformative experiences in prison. There is an incredible opportunity to use the wisdom and hindsight these men already have about their lives to build up and out of the oppressive disciplinary constraints that the cognitive self-change program uses to bind them now. What is needed is a catalyst for this transformation. Policy revision based upon a redefinition of expert knowledge favoring the inmates as the ones most knowledgeable of their own struggles, obstacles and abilities creates that opportunity.

Lived realities

Rather than denying inmates' pasts or disciplining them for articulating their unique experiences, the insights gained from the analysis of their own lives can become the site of a new institutional agenda. Such an agenda *privileges* the personal stories and struggles expressed by the inmates and suggests functional recommendations for action based on real problems and lived realities. Maintaining the principle of responsibility is possible by using a collaborative model that includes understanding the influences of other people and circumstances in tandem with recognizing one's own role in the variety of choices and decisions faced. Rather than insisting that the inmates can and should change their pasts, redefining what taking responsibility means can reconcile the difficulties they face. Allowing for the possibility of joint responsibility as it is dispersed among many different actors, institutions and circumstances will bring the inmates into a realm of better understanding their place in the social environment outside prison. Instructing the inmates how to *ask* for help, rather than insisting that only they can help themselves, is a much more realistic and far more functional application of taking responsibility.

Understanding how others can influence their lives both positively and negatively allows the inmates to engage in the process of identifying how responsibility can be shared. Reflecting on past mistakes as well as past successes and future struggles can also be redefined as a way to be responsible. The suggested changes here do not devalue the principles of cognitive-behavioral therapy, the goals of the institution or the insights of prison administrators and staff. Instead, they bring the inmates themselves up to a place of personal empowerment and allow them a stake in their own learning and transformative experiences.

Making choices

In its redefinition of expert knowledge, the institution can also acknowledge the myriad possibilities involved in making choices. Instead of only addressing examples that provide a good choice and a bad choice, realistically including scenarios the inmates may face where the dilemma is between making a bad choice or another bad choice can refocus the problem onto the *process* of decision making rather than on the actual choice itself.

Everyday problems are wrought with possibilities for action and rarely do people encounter a situation that yields only one choice. By refocusing the direction of the prison's programs onto the individual analysis of the elements of the process of making decisions, the institution can more fully prepare the inmates for life after prison. Making powerful decisions has much more to do with understanding how one comes to those decisions than does the rightness or wrongness of a particular behavior. Realistically addressing this basic element of decision making doesn't undermine the prison; rather, it educates the inmates.

Asking the inmates themselves to share their own examples of difficult decisions they had to make or worrisome obstacles they anticipate in the future is a way of empowering them to engage in self- and other-awareness. Those stories and experiences they tell, then, are the expert knowledge; they are the building blocks that make up the lived realities. Redefining what counts as expert knowledge can lead to the inmates' investment in the program. It is likely then that if the inmates feel that they have made a unique and personal contribution toward their future the outcome may be more emancipatory than a struggle with constraint. By deciding for themselves what they think and feel, rather than having the authorities tell them what is acceptable to think and feel, the inmates gain a vested interest in themselves and in the program.

Redefining the experts as the inmates themselves destroys the one-size-fits-all meta-narrative of the prison and replaces it with a patchwork of individual narratives, linked by similarities and differences through self-investment. The goal then, becomes altered from encouraging the inmates to change their thinking patterns to empowering them to overcome their own personal struggles. In the process of individually identifying what they have done well, instead of being forced to admit what they did wrong, the inmates can work toward repeating past successes and recognizing their application in the future as the key to reaching goals they set.

Players and roles

If meanings become redefined, then the role of justice administrators must also change. Rather than "instructors" teaching the inmates how to change their thinking patterns, a new focus would be on facilitators providing guidance through collaboration. The inmates rely on one another to share their experiences and receive validation and support. An atmosphere that emphasizes support, rather than blame and respect over degradation, provides a much more conducive environment for the application of personal investment. The group facilitators can focus on the applicability of the inmates' stories to functional solutions in the future, instead of simply assigning a value judgment to their thoughts and feelings.

As facilitators in these classes, rather than instructors or administrators, the prison staff can engage both the authoritative element necessary to successfully running a prison and also act as a conductor through which the inmates funnel their experiences, issues, fears and decisions. In redefining the role of the staff in the particular venue of the weekly prison class, the shared space can become a safer space. In many of the narratives gathered for this book, the inmates longed to be able to tell their stories to someone willing to listen. If they are allowed to openly express themselves, rather than being shut down for giving a wrong answer, the inmates may begin to see their own lives reflected in the stories of others. The shared experiences then open the door to shared solutions and solutions are certainly what the Department of Corrections claims to want.

Collaborative possibilities

During my interviews with the thirty inmates in this study, the single most frequently occurring concern they articulated was uncertainty. They were as uncertain about what they would do their first few hours after release as they were about whether or not they would return to prison in a year. This expression of uncertainty indicates that, perhaps, they aren't as invested in the process of recovery and transition as they could be. It seems that someone who had truly been helped and who managed to change their flawed thinking (the thing that allegedly led them to prison in the first place) would have a much more optimistic vision of their own future than do these men. The issue is they are as at odds with the institution as the institution is with them. There are clear sides in prison, and the inmates are always disadvantaged. One way for inmates to begin to become invested in their own recovery and feel more certain about the future of their lives is to engage in partnership with the institution, rather than a battle.

One way to begin constructing a collaborative recidivism reduction program is to gather panels of current and ex-offenders in order to garner their ideas and cultivate their experiences and needs to form a brand new program. The best way to determine how to help someone is to ask them what they need. There is no more learned an expert on recidivism than someone who has gone through it. Using these stories and experiences to create the content of a new class serves multiple functions. First, it lends credibility to the content in the program, which may encourage future inmates to pay closer attention or put more stock into the class. If the inmates believe that the material they receive is based in the realities of inmates who came before them, they will likely be much more receptive.

Second, using inmates as the architects of a new program serves the purpose of better linking the exercises and examples in the class to those the inmates will likely face on release. One of the most confounding aspects of the 'Pathway to Change' class was that the examples provided for the inmates to consider were impractical and unrealistic. By using real, tangible, historical examples from the individuals who struggled in the past to mold a new program, the class gains the validity and applicability it previously lacked.

Third, gathering the suggestions of ex-inmates in the formation of a new in-prison program will allow the program to be based on respect and mutual understanding. Having served time in prison previously, the ex-inmates helping create the new class have a first-hand perspective of the degradation and shame inherent in prison (Maruna, 2008). Their insights into the language, activities, examples and solutions posed in the new class will prove invaluable in gauging the appropriateness of the new exercises and assignments. Further, as ex-inmates, these individuals would still likely be in the process of negotiating their lives post-release. Their continued recovery could benefit from their involvement in the creation and production of classes they know will be used to help others like them. Continued investment and support can continue for these men on the outside.

Fourth, in addition to creating steering committees of current and ex-inmates as a way to inform the production of a new prison class, distributing anonymous entrance and exit surveys in current mandatory prison classes could help the institution determine the program's strengths and weaknesses. Conducting in-depth interviews with current inmates that assess their actual and perceived needs and challenges upon release is another way to begin the process of building a collaborative model. Taking into account the complex relationship of the inmates to elements beyond their immediate control does not necessarily open the door to blaming others. Rather, it enables an ideological shift on both the part of the inmates as well as the institution to acknowledge the complicated and nuanced realities that exist in the "real world." Anonymous or confidential entrance and exit surveys used to assess the strengths and weaknesses of in-prison programs serve as an internal check to ensure that good work is being done.

Without qualitatively reevaluating the elements in existing policy, the prison system allows dysfunctional programs like 'Pathway to Change' to continue. Essential to program reform is the evaluative component, determining if the measures currently in place are actually working. Studies on prison programs designed to reduce recidivism show that the programs most successful in accomplishing their goals are those that differentiate their treatment plans for substance abuse and sexual-offender targets (Wormith et al., 2007). The 'Pathway to Change' program was administered to a variety of offenders who were chosen to participate in the Missouri Reentry Process. Without regard for their individual needs, the crimes for which they were convicted or their risk level, the inmates in this study were chosen to participate in the class based on the time remaining on their respective sentences. In fact, of the thirty inmates interviewed in this study, almost all had experienced substance abuse issues and several were convicted sex-offenders. The potential to separate types of offenders and provide treatment situated in a more needs-based premise is promising. This type of separation does not require any additional resource or money from the state. The attempt to create a universally applicable recidivism-reduction course in prison on the basis of time served is illogical and goes against significant research findings that indicate the most successful cognitive-based programs help reduce recidivism primarily in courses based on individualized and specific offender risk, need and responsivity assessment (Andrews et al., 2006).

Asking the inmates to invest their own time, ideas, opinions and perspectives about their lives may allow them to take a much more vested approach to how they can work the program and, in turn, may help make them more successful at staying out of prison in the future (Maruna, 2008; Stevens, 2013). In the field of Social Work, these types of holistic approaches are called "anti-oppressive practices," wherein a full overview of possible difficulties facing clients is taken into consideration (Pollack, 2004). This type of treatment is predicated on the idea that people in need of social aid are suffering as a result of systemic problems, not just personal ones. Researchers doing work with offenders' oral histories use a similar tactic in their own interviewing methodologies called "reciprocal ethnography," wherein the processes of interpretation and analysis of the stories are shared by the researcher and the participant (Rouverol, 2003).

For Alicia Rouverol (2003), collaboration in a correctional setting is uniquely challenging because it goes against the very essence of the prison place to begin with. Collaboration requires the inmates to redefine their own roles as authority figures. Many of the inmates she interviewed found the process of self-redefinition difficult because "collaboration – whether with each other or with us – also meant building trust, a rare commodity in a prison setting" (77). In any case, collaborative projects in a prison are certain to present significant challenges. However, if researchers, program designers and policy makers can begin from the premise that inmates are capable and willing to engage in self-reflexivity, then efforts can be made to work toward the mutual, reciprocal and shared construction of new programs in which the inmates can invest. The crux of the issue is, I argue, in redefining what is meant by "expert knowledge." Privileging the inmates as the experts opens up whole new ways of designing programs and new bases for exploring the use of these collaborative techniques in prison.

Alisa Steven's 2013 study found that the use of therapeutic communities in prisons, as an alternative to cognitive-behavioral programs, contributed to a significant reduction in recidivism. The premise of therapeutic prison communities used in England and Wales focuses on group therapies lead by prisoners, the development of positive self-concepts, ownership of one's ability to overcome hardship and the support and understanding of other inmates and staff. According to Stevens (2013, 168):

> For all of the uncertainties surrounding TCs – to what extent they work, how they work, and, in darker moments, concerns about whether they will endure – one cannot ignore that, for some people, the prison-based TC, with its self-esteem enhancing, strengths-based, and hope-inducing rehabilitative regime, can provide the hook for change upon which to hang a new, transformed version of oneself.

The notion of collaborative practices in institutional programming is embedded in the much larger considerations of critical theory in general (Dryzek, 1987). Discursive projects that attempt to break down existing dialogues in favor of those unique stories of experience that have been diffused into a common meta-narrative speak to the type of change necessary for the growth of collaborative techniques in organizations. Criticism of the whole of the criminal justice system likewise takes root in similar beginnings. For Wacquant (2009, xii),

> the law-and-order-merry-go-round is to criminality what pornography is to amorous relations: a mirror deforming reality to the point of the

> grotesque that artificially extracts delinquent behaviors from the fabric of social relations in which they take root and make sense, deliberately ignores their causes and their meanings, and reduces their treatment to a series of conspicuous position-takings.

Disengaging from the discourse of dominant rationality is a task that is essential to the project of creating humanistic revisions in institutional settings (Polizzi & Braswell, 2009). By questioning the premises upon which these very social policies are based, we allow a critical engagement with the dominant discourse to flourish. For Thomas McLaughlin (1996), "those premises could be thought of as servants of power, producing what seemed like truth but functioned as strategies of manipulation" (29). For Polizzi et al. (2013), the key to fighting those strategies of manipulation in prison lies in "re-subjectifying" policy. Here, the authors explain that current polices refuse to acknowledge the contradictory nature of what is expected of the inmates and the realities of their ability to put those expectations into practice after release. Reconstituting the institutional expectations of the inmates in a way that brings subjectivity back into prison policy brings a level of humanism and an active engagement to the role of policy-makers as well as to the inmates. The authors contend that introducing subjectivity into prison policies would mean that policy-makers must first admit that their previous understandings of inmates' lived realities were flawed and that they are willing to work with the inmates (rather than against them) in re-defining what is important, what is possible for them to achieve and what may stand in their way. Remaining engaged in the critical evaluation of every nuanced aspect of a problem reveals far more than its momentary articulation as problematic; it also reveals its place in a multi-layered system of socially constructed premises where one flawed assumption infects all that follow.

Righting wrongs through programmatic reform

One of the primary problems with the 'Pathway to Change' class was in the way it was implemented. Prison staff members, who are not trained or licensed psychologists or counselors, administer the course after completing six hours of training provided by the Missouri Department of Corrections. They teach from the instructor's copy of the handbook and are left to their own discretion which lessons to teach, how to teach them, how to grade the inmates and whether or not participants pass the class (and, ultimately, whether or not the inmates are released from prison). The issue of improper training can be eliminated if the program model shifted to a more inmate-driven course. Prison staff would not need to be trained in the methods and techniques of psychology to lead the class because they would no longer be charged with changing inmates' flawed thinking patterns. Rather, staff members would serve to funnel and filter discussions based around particular real-world topics relevant to the inmates in the class at the time. Their role would be to provide structure, rather than manipulate thoughts, and facilitate discussion, rather than assign value to the answers inmates give. In this way, prison staff act as conductors rather than teachers, so the time and money spent training them how to teach cognitive-behavioral psychology can be spent instead teaching them active listening techniques, ways to facilitate a safe discussion space and how to draw out meaning from contested narratives in a group setting.

Similarly, another significant flaw in the 'Pathway to Change' class could be eliminated through program revision. The fact that passing the course is a mandatory condition of inmates' ultimate release from prison makes it impossible for the instructors and the state to know how and if the program works. Do the inmates internalize the lessons' objectives, or simply repeat the language in the course to the satisfaction of the instructor? Is the class a key component in the entire reentry process, or simply a hoop through which the inmates know they must jump? These questions are impossible to answer as the program stands now. In order to assess the extent to which psychology-based programs work, implementers of the programs must listen to their participants for feedback. In 'Pathway to Change,' attempts to speak outside the bounds of the prescribed structure of the lessons are characterized as "incorrect" answers. In this way, determining how the inmates feel about the content or whether they accept it at all is impossible.

Certainly, on a very real level everything in prison is mandatory. There is little free will or rational choice involved in anything the inmates do, let alone which programs they will take or how they will use them. Particularly, in a class like 'Pathway to Change,' which is just one piece to a larger process, the inmates are not at leisure to decline participation when their freedom is on the line. However, in a reformed program the process of engaging in a class about decision making and life choices could be considered one of several available options required for release. If the inmates are allowed some agency in their own choices about recovery and transition, it may be the case that they will find themselves much more engaged and invested in the courses they take. Holding one particular class over their heads as bait for getting out of prison seems counterintuitive to the principles and theories upon which the reentry process is based.

Finally, program reform in prison from classes like 'Pathway to Change' would necessarily involve phasing out tactics that could marginalize and disrespect inmates as people. These men are not unintelligent degenerates who need to be talked down to in order to understand issues related to their own lives. These men are fathers and sons who had lives before prison and who will have a life when they get out. Dehumanizing them by using techniques designed to train unruly children is grossly unnecessary and could, in fact, have lasting negative effects on their conceptions of self and others. The purpose of a reformed program focused toward decision making and successful transition out of prison would be to encourage and support them so they can walk out with certainty and confidence in their ability to stay out.

By addressing these three issues, training of prison staff members and program implementation, mandatory requirements of release and the marginalizing aspects of current programs, new, better in-prison recidivism-reduction programs can be put into place and generated by the inmates themselves. The suggestions made here are not radical, nor are they impossible to implement. These are practical empirically based critiques of one prison program that can be improved upon in order to produce a more just and cooperative experience for those it affects.

The issue for this project has never been whether or not cognitive-behavioral based prison classes and the Missouri Reentry Process work to reduce recidivism; they do. The issue has been to ask: at what cost to the inmates do they accomplish that goal?

Moving forward

My challenge with this work is in upholding the tenets of critical theory while creating a realistic proposal for change that speaks the language of justice administrators. Time, money and efficiency are a large part of what matters in one of the largest state-run bureaucratic enterprises. State Departments of Correction claim to want to reduce recidivism. They also claim to want to achieve this goal at the lowest cost to taxpayers. Creating change in such a structure will require persistence and an understanding of bureaucratic constraints. Recidivism rates continue to rise, and so reducing them continues to be a state goal. It is essential that a new program of collaboration remains anchored in the understanding that it must realistically exist at no additional cost, time or burden to the agents of the institution. Reducing the risk to the institution and the state is absolutely essential to proposing these changes and, I believe, entirely realistic. Where one program exists, another can be born to replace it. The current program is inherently and irreparably flawed. It consists of a network that uses self-blame, degradation, detachment from reality, disconnectedness and expert knowledge to discursively discipline inmates by imposing a definitive meta-narrative. Departments of Correction use this and similar programs across the country and continue to invest the time, energy and resources of prison staff into their perpetuation. The same time, energy and resources currently expended on a dysfunctional program could be rerouted and invigorated through a new experience-based class that engages the lived realities of current and ex-inmates in the production of a new kind of expert knowledge. The money spent on contracting out programs like 'Pathway to Change' could be spent contracting out a better program. The dollars spent on maintaining instructor's manuals and staff training can just as easily be spent on printing and training for a new program.

It is my sincere belief that researchers endeavoring upon such a project will have no trouble whatsoever finding current and ex-inmates willing to contribute to the content of a new class. In fact, the inmates I interviewed jumped at the chance to provide their suggestions for improvement:

BILL: It seems like the people who are on the right path already have someone to listen to them.

JOSEPH: You need people who've been in and out of prison to counsel them. The younger kids in here respect the older ones. But, you'll have to have success stories.

JAMES: [It would help if] you'd get to talk to someone who doesn't judge. You build up a lot of stuff in here; it'd be nice to get it out. You don't feel like you can talk to nobody in here. This stuff I just told you I wouldn't have told to anyone. This conversation we're having right here will stick with me because you didn't judge.

HAROLD: The more productive classes help with resumes and checkbooks and job interviews. But the other ones – they take the classes out of context of real life. They say they're giving us the tools to live, but experience is the best teacher. It'd be nice to see ex-offenders run those types of programs. Just share how they took the first step. The most successful programs on the outside have to do with ex-offenders. You can't teach life out of a book.

My goal with this book has been to tie my analyses as closely to the data as possible, and so too do I tie my suggestions for policy reform in prison to these inmates' narratives. The conclusions and suggestions provided here aren't novel; in fact, they aren't even my own. The inmates are asking for these changes and it is our obligation as researchers, activists and promoters of social justice to take them seriously.

Future research connecting the discursive realities as narrated by inmates and their relationship to in-prison programs and policies designed to reduce recidivism is essential to creating change. More research on cognitive self-change classes across a variety of institutions and how they affect the storied pasts, presents and futures of their members is necessary to further our understanding of these complex relationships. The redefinition of expert knowledge as lived realities is key in the weakening of programs like 'Pathway to Change.' These programs impose such an oppressive and damaging form of institutional discipline by monopolizing the potentialities of all discursive practices that, as evidenced by this research, the people they claim to be helping are, at best, ambiguous about their chances of succeeding in a future that no longer belongs to them.

References

Andrews, D. A., Bonta, J. & Wormith, J. S. (2006). The recent past and near future of risk and/or need assessment. *Crime & Delinquency, 52*, 7–27.

Dryzek, J. S. (1987). Discursive designs: Critical theory and political institutions. *American Journal of Political Science, 31*(3), 656–79.

McLaughlin, T. (1996). *Street Smarts and Critical Theory: Listening to the Vernacular.* Madison: University of Wisconsin Press.

Maruna, S. (2008). *Making good: How ex-convicts reform and rebuild their lives.* Washington, DC: American Psychological Association.
Polizzi, D. & Braswell, M. (2009). *Transforming corrections: Humanistic approaches to corrections and offender treatment.* Durham, NC: Carolina Academic Press.
Polizzi, D., Draper, M. & Anderson, M. (2013). Fabricated selves and the rehabilitative machine: Toward a phenomenology of the social construction of offender treatment. In B. A. Arrigo & H. Y. Bersot (Eds.), *The Routledge handbook of international crime and justice studies.* New York and London: Routledge.
Pollack, S. (2004). Anti-oppressive social work practice with women in prison: Discursive reconstruction and alternative practices. *British Journal of Social Work, 34,* 693–707.
Rouverol, A. J. (2003). Collaborative oral history in a correctional setting: Promise and pitfalls. *The Oral History Review, 30*(1), 61–85.
Stevens, A. (2013). *Offender rehabilitation and therapeutic communities: Enabling change the TC way.* New York: Routledge.
Wacquant, L. J. D. (2009). *Punishing the poor: The neoliberal government of social insecurity.* Durham, NC: Duke University Press.
Wormith, S. J., Althouse, R., Simpson, M., Reitzel, L. R., Fagan, T. J. & Morgan, R. D. (2007). The rehabilitation and reintegration of offenders: The current landscape and some future directions for correctional psychology. *Criminal Justice and Behavior, 34*(7), 879–92.

Index

For Product Safety Concerns and Information please contact our EU representative GPSR@taylorandfrancis.com Taylor & Francis Verlag GmbH, Kaufingerstraße 24, 80331 München, Germany